WALT'S DISNEYLAND

A Walk in the Park with Walt Disney

Marcy Carriker Smothers

EDITIONS

Los Angeles · New York

THIS BOOK IS DEDICATED TO DISNEY LEGEND
JIM CORA, MY MENTOR AND MY FRIEND

I wrote this book in Walt's folksy style. With simplicity in mind, I combined quotes culled from hundreds of sources, including the Walt Disney Archives, Walt Disney Archives Photo Library, Imagineering Resource Center, Walt Disney Imagineering Photo Collection, museums, books, newspaper articles, magazines, souvenir guides, vintage television shows, documentaries, and interviews. Everyone in this book knew Walt; it was important for me to use only first-person accounts. And just as Walt was on a first-name basis, I kept titles and role descriptions to a minimum. If you'd like to learn more about the people who helped Walt create Disneyland— and the origins of their stories—please refer to Dream Doers and Endnotes.

—MARCY CARRIKER SMOTHERS

"Walt used to say that Disneyland would never be finished, and it never will. I like to think, too, that Walt Disney's influence will never be finished; that through his creations, future generations will continue to celebrate what he once described as 'that precious, ageless something in every human being which makes us play with children's toys and laugh at silly things and sing in the bathtub and dream.'"

—ROY O. DISNEY

> **"And I kept insisting I wanted this amusement park. And everybody says, '[What's] he want that . . . amusement park for?' And I couldn't think up a good reason except that . . . I don't know, I wanted it."**
> —WALT

He drove through the Harbor Boulevard employees' gate and parked. Entering from backstage, he walked briskly across Town Square to his apartment above the firehouse.

Operations supervisors' radios were instantly abuzz: CODE W!

Walt Disney was in Disneyland.

He was in his happy place. His playhouse. An impresario in his own show.

The theme park he created, played in, and sometimes lived in. Where he drove his fire truck, engineered his train, and piloted the *Mark Twain*. Where he sailed the world and soared over London. Climbed a tree house and descended in a submarine. Roared in laughter at the Golden Horseshoe and tapped his toes at the bandstand. Where Walt proudly put his right hand over his heart during the flag retreat in his small American town.

The gift he gave the world keeps on giving.

There is only one Grand Canyon. One Leaning Tower of Pisa. One Great Wall of China. And only one Disneyland.

"I've always said there will never be another Disneyland, and I think it's going to work out that way."

Walking with Walt, you'll see Disneyland through his eyes, his heart, and his words. Walt's magic remains in his Magic Kingdom.

PAGE 1: *Walt's #1 badge was long believed to be lost; however, Disney archivist Ed Ovalle never lost sight of this precious piece of Disneyland history. While Ed's primary research focus is Walt Disney, one afternoon he decided to look through Roy O. Disney's files. In the very back of a box, he noticed a crumpled paper bag that was displacing the folders. He shook it and it sounded like metal. Inside, along with some Donald Duck pins, was Walt's badge. His brother had saved it among his personal items; it was neither lost nor forgotten.* **PAGES 2–3:** *The Kalamazoo handcar was installed on the former passing track in 1957 and was a part of Walt's private collection. While I was writing* Eat Like Walt, *Marty Sklar and Jim Cora confirmed it was shot in August 1966 by Renie Bardeau. Research for this book, however, points to October 14, 1966, and the grainy photo (page 158) generously provided by the Congressional Medal of Honor Society, as an even later shot taken of Walt in his beloved Magic Kingdom.* **OPPOSITE:** *Walt with Disneyland aerial overview painting and model, 1954.*

CONTENTS

Walt on the set of his lead-in for Disneyland, U.S.A. *at Radio City Music Hall, 1962.*

CHAPTER ONE
BEFORE DISNEYLAND

"By the time Walt gets through, this will not only be the seventh wonder of the world, but the eighth, ninth and tenth as well."

— TIME MAGAZINE

SETTING THE SCENE: SEPTEMBER 26–27, 1953

W alt had been thinking about his "amusement" park off and on for twenty years. Now it was closer than ever to reality. He needed someone to help him transform what was in his imagination—what he had been dreaming about all those years—into something visual: an overall concept drawing.

Herb Ryman was his man. Herbie, as he was affectionately known, was an art director on *Dumbo* and *Fantasia*. Walt admired his sketching ability and storytelling. He called the artist on September 26, 1953.

Herb describes that fateful Saturday:

"'Hi, Herbie, I'm over here at the studio. I wonder if you could come over here. Just come the way you are. I'll be out front waiting for you.'

"I was curious, and flattered that he picked up the phone and called me. I had no idea what he wanted.

"He met me out front and shook my hand, saying, 'Hi, Herbie.' So we went in, and I asked what this was all about. He said, 'Well, we're going to do an amusement park.'

"I said, 'That's good and exciting. So what do you want to see me about?'

"He said, 'My brother Roy has to go to New York on Monday morning. He's got to talk to some bankers there. You know bankers don't have any imagination, none at all. You have to show them what you're going to do. Roy has to show them what this place is going to look like.'

"And I said, 'Well, I'd like to see what this place is going to look like, too. Where have you got all this stuff?' I thought maybe it was in the other room.

"Walt said, 'You're going to do it.'

"I said, 'No I'm not.'

"Walt paced around the room with his arms folded, kind of paced back and forth, then went over and stood in the corner, kind of looked back at me over his left shoulder with a kind of sheepish smile, like a boy who really wants something.

"This whole area was just an orange grove and some farmhouses . . . I was pacing this place off . . . it took a lot of pacing. It was over two hundred acres," said Walt as he surveyed the land that would become his Magic Kingdom.

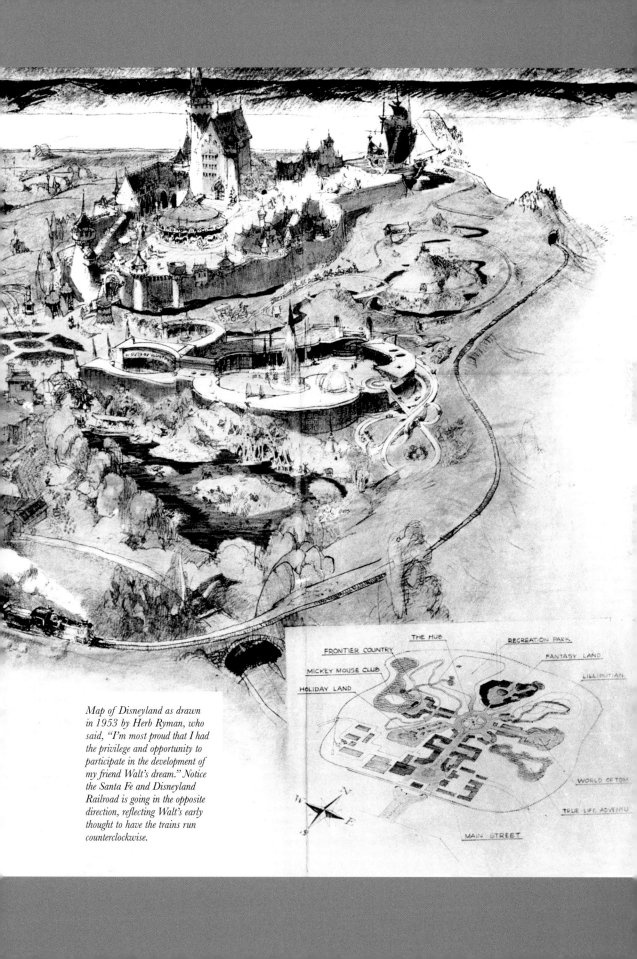

Map of Disneyland as drawn in 1953 by Herb Ryman, who said, "I'm most proud that I had the privilege and opportunity to participate in the development of my friend Walt's dream." Notice the Santa Fe and Disneyland Railroad is going in the opposite direction, reflecting Walt's early thought to have the trains run counterclockwise.

THE HUB

FRONTIER COUNTRY

RECREATION PARK

FANTASY LAND

MICKEY MOUSE CLUB

LILLIPUTIAN

HOLIDAY LAND

WORLD OF TOM

TRUE-LIFE ADVENTU

MAIN STREET

N

W E

S

> **"Walt restlessly prowls the earth like a walking electronic computer storing up data. You never know when he's going to press a button, and some idea, maybe from as far back as 1910, will come tumbling out of his brain."**
>
> —CHARLES LEVY

"With his eyes brimming, he asked, 'Herbie, will you do it if I stay here with you?'

"I began to think, 'Well, he's very serious about this,' and Walt, after all, was my friend, so I said, 'Sure, if you stay here all night tonight and all night Sunday and help me, I'll stay here and see what I can do.'"

Walt and Herb worked together throughout the weekend and finished late on Sunday evening. The next morning Roy was on a plane to see the bankers.

And the rest is living history.

Walt needed to choose the ideal location for his big idea. He hired the Stanford Research Institute to investigate. In his first meeting with Walt, economist Harrison "Buzz" Price asked, "Do you have any bias, any opinion, on where it should go in Southern California? The study area you are talking about is big. The greater Los Angeles five-county area is at least four thousand square miles. The eight-county area is even larger."

"No, you tell me," Walt said firmly.

"You own the Golden Oak Ranch in Saugus. Is that a consideration?" Buzz probed.

"No, you tell me where it should go," Walt reiterated.

And with those marching orders and extensive research, Buzz concluded, "All in all, the data seemed to zero in on an area we called the amoeba because of its irregular shape. It was five miles either side of the Santa Ana Freeway from the L.A. County line to Santa Ana . . . Walt and Roy agreed with our approach and went after the first-choice site, an orange grove at the intersection of the Santa Ana Freeway and Harbor Boulevard. Later the site was moved one quarter mile to the south, away from the freeway."

"I first saw the site for Disneyland back in 1953," explained Walt. "In those days, it was all flat land—no rivers, no mountains, no castles or rocket ships—just orange groves and a few acres of walnut trees. Anaheim was a town of fourteen thousand then, and if someone had mentioned that one year soon, six million visitors would come to Disneyland, folks might have had second thoughts about inviting us. In fact, we might have had second thoughts about building a Disneyland!"

"When he started Disneyland, I thought, 'How can he? This is something nobody has ever done,'" recalled Walt's wife, Lilly. "There is no pattern to follow. How can you do it? But somehow, he had, and all within his own organization, you see. He pulled this all together and he went out and got good people. But how did they know how to do that? Without any experience?"

Walt's daughter Diane Disney Miller reminisces: "Originally he thought of Disneyland as an amusement park covering perhaps one city block. But his plans kept growing. His conversation about it at home became so sweeping that I didn't take him seriously. He spoke of a fairyland castle, and a real steamboat on a real river that would represent all the rivers in the world. I didn't think those things were possible. Even when I went out to the Disneyland site at Anaheim, twenty-eight miles southeast of Los Angeles, and saw them shoving mountains around, I couldn't believe it was going to come true. Yet Dad made it come true."

Walt sums it up: "This dream really started to come to life in July 1954, when the

"The name Imagineering was suggested to Walt in an early meeting by Buzz Price, the economist who recommended the sites in Anaheim and Orlando for Disneyland and Walt Disney World, respectively. The term combines *imagination* with *engineering*—thus *imagineering*. Walt liked it immediately. To assure Buzz received proper credit for the name, Walt sent him a letter in the 1960s thanking him for the suggestion."

—MARTY SKLAR

bulldozers moved in and started leveling the site. To build our Magic Kingdom took more than a magic wand; it took earthmovers. This was no place for a man with a hand shovel. Scooping out lakes and broad riverbeds paid off in enough dirt for rolling hills, islands, and mountains. There was an opening date to meet and time was running out. Men and machines shifted into high gear. Work progressed at a fast pace. *Unbelievably* fast. The tempo was terrific, but the carpenters were on the beat. Rome could have been built in a day if these crews had been on that job. After many hectic, yet happy weeks, the big day arrived. On July 17, 1955, we opened the gates to all people from all over the world to enjoy this Magic Kingdom with us."

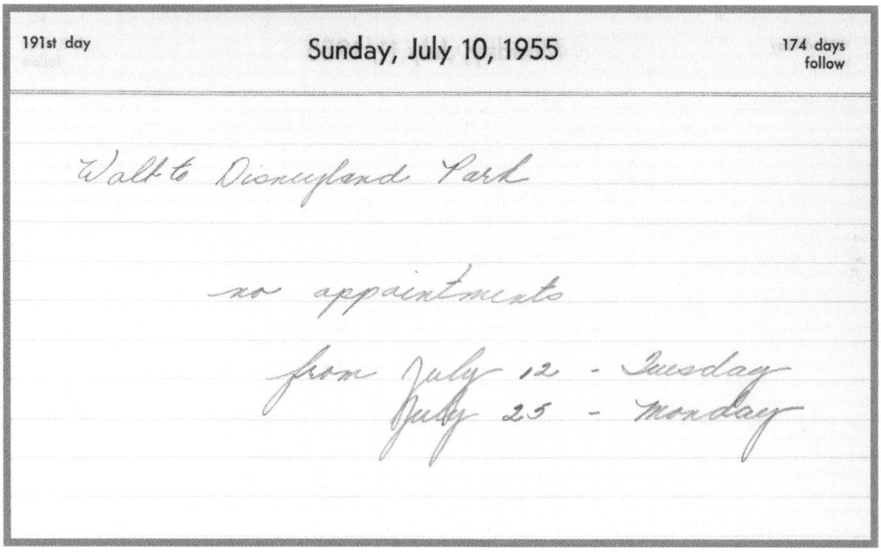

191st day

Sunday, July 10, 1955

174 days follow

Walt to Disneyland Park

no appointments

from July 12 - Tuesday
July 25 - Monday

Walt's edict entered in his personal desk diary that he would be focusing solely on Disneyland in preparation for its opening on July 17, 1955: "Walt to Disneyland Park. No appointments from July 12, Tuesday to July 25, Monday."

"The key to Walt's approach to any kind of design was to consider the environment that was being created for people. He said, 'All I want you to think about is when people walk or ride through anything you design, I want them to have smiles on their faces when they leave. Just remember that and that's all I ask you.'"

—MARVIN DAVIS

CHAPTER TWO
OUTSIDE DISNEYLAND

"For all the people that will visit us, their arrival at Disneyland is the fulfillment of planning and dreaming of visiting the Magic Kingdom. To us, every one of these guests is a VIP–Very Important Person."

—WALT

Walt valued every guest and made sure they felt appreciated from the very beginning of their visit. He understood that the first impression of Disneyland was made when vehicles entered the property. He believed the parking process was the vital first experience; thus his lots were clean and secure. He knew that his guests wouldn't feel safe if their vehicles weren't safe.

If it's possible, Walt (and his handpicked team) thought of *everything*.

Notice the souvenir stand outside the gates before you enter the original Magic Kingdom. That's a Walt touch dating back to 1955. Disneyland was closed on various Mondays and Tuesdays for cleaning and maintenance (part of Walt's high standards); however, Walt didn't want guests to be upset if they didn't know that and arrived at Disneyland on the first two days of the week. The stand was open and ready for business, selling hats, trinkets, toys, maps, and memorabilia. That way, Walt knew, guests wouldn't be terribly disappointed and would have something to take home from Disneyland.

A lover of all animals, Walt also had plans for the furry friends of his guests: "We're building a Dogland, where people can leave their dogs to be cared for while they're in the park." He wanted to be sure all pets would be safe—and not in hot cars—while their owners were enjoying Disneyland.

"Disneyland itself is the one place in the world that Walt personally designed and then had maybe eleven years to work around and form it, so I use the expression that it's the road map of Walt Disney's life or mind."

—VAN FRANCE

Walt with Disneyland-Alweg Monorail extension under construction. Initially only an attraction inside Tomorrowland, it was extended to include transportation to the Disneyland Hotel in 1961.

> **"Disneyland is a state of mind. Disneyland is not only a place in Anaheim; it's a place to be entertained, intrigued. It's not merely just a place to go; it's something to become part of—if only for a day."**
>
> —WALT

The ticket booths, of course, are also found here. Walt believed in value when it came to pricing. As Dick Nunis recalls Walt telling his operations team: "Look, let's not be concerned when a guest comes to the gate and says, 'Why do I have to pay to get in?' Let's be concerned with two things when they leave. Number one: did they have fun? And number two: did they receive their value? Because people will pay for quality."

As you approach the gates, it's worth noting that Walt wanted only one entrance and one exit. They are the same.

"The overall shape of the park, with its single entrance, was Walt's, and that was the key to the whole thing," explains Disneyland designer and Imagineer Marvin Davis. "Walt was very circulation conscious, and he wanted a single entrance so that they could control the number of people that came in, and know the number that went out, and know what's in the park."

"One time he came over to my house. He asked if I wanted to go to the Fairmount Amusement Park. I told him I had no money," said William Rast, Walt's childhood friend from Kansas City. "He said we didn't need any, as he knew how to sneak in . . . we went over to where the entrance to the Fairmount was. We carefully watched, looked around . . . there was this big screen, which some other kids had already opened. We just pushed it over and snuck in. We spent the whole day there. He made me promise never to tell the story when he was alive. He thought kids might use the excuse that if he could do it, then they could try to get into his park without paying."

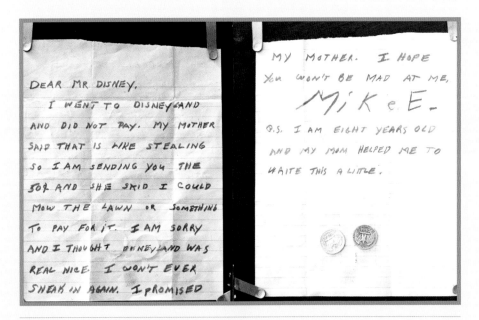

Indeed, decades later, a young boy snuck into Walt's park. A copy of this apology letter and recompense for the admission fee has been preserved in the Walt Disney Archives.

TOP: *Walt at the* Disneyland News *newstand that used to sit outside Disneyland, 1956.* BOTTOM: *Concept art for the souvenir stand Walt had installed outside Disneyland's gates.*

Ken-L Land Pet Motel (for the sponsor Ken-L Ration) opened in 1958. In 1968 it was renamed Kennel Club, when Kal Kan became the sponsor until 1977. Gaines sponsored the facility—Pet Care Kennel—from 1986 to 1991. When Friskies took over in 1993, the Kennel Club name returned. Today it operates as the Disneyland Resort Kennel Club.

CHAPTER THREE

THE GRAND ENTRANCE

> **"One thing that surprises me
> is how early they arrive."**
>
> —WALT

A s you move through the turnstiles, you're entering Disneyland's lobby. Guests are greeted by a giant floral Mickey Mouse, and Walt reminds us:

"The story of Mickey is truthfully the real beginning of Disneyland."

Above that are the Disneyland Railroad and Main Street Station. The railroad sits on a twenty-foot berm (a mound of earth or raised barrier) that surrounds the park. That was Walt's way of keeping his guests immersed in the magic while keeping the outside world—with its troubles and realities—out. It was also Walt's intention that the train station serve as Disneyland's marquee, and in that role, it needed elevation to grab attention.

While his film audiences traditionally stayed firmly in their seats, Walt wanted his guests to participate in the show: "In a sense, Disneyland is a stage—a most unusual stage. Members of the Disneyland audience, unlike the audience at a motion picture or Broadway show, do not simply look on. They participate in the drama, adventure, or comedy. They walk onto the stage. They move through the sets. They touch the props . . . Disneyland is the star: everything else is in the supporting role."

Before you pass under either side of the railroad tracks, Walt's words welcome you:

*"Here you leave today and enter the world of
yesterday, tomorrow and fantasy."*

Showtime!

> **"Fill this place with people, and
> you'll really have a show."**
>
> —WALT

Walt with workers, circa 1955.

This photo was taken prior to Opening Day, thus the Floral Mickey is framed but not yet planted. "Population 5,000,000" is a mystery, since Disneyland had not opened its gates yet!

CHAPTER FOUR

TOWN SQUARE

"To all who come to this happy place: Welcome. Disneyland is your land. Here age relives fond memories of the past—and here youth may savor the challenge and promise of the future. Disneyland is dedicated to the ideals, the dreams, and the hard facts that have created America—with the hope that it will be a source of joy and inspiration to all the world."

—JULY 17, 1955

Later, in souvenir guidebooks, Walt welcomed his guests with this suggestion: "During your visit, you may wish to stop for a moment in Town Square. There, at the base of the flagpole, you will find a message which expresses Disneyland's true purpose." The original plaque with Walt's dedication speech remains in that place of honor.

SANTA FE AND DISNEYLAND RAILROAD AND MAIN STREET STATION (1955)
Los Angeles Times columnist Hedda Hopper, who was quite chummy with Walt, shared her experiences at Disneyland on July 16, the day before it opened to a preview audience: "First thing we saw on entering the park was a floral replica of Mickey Mouse. And there was his creator, Disney himself, manning the controls of the tiny train that circles the park. 'All aboard!' he yelled as he grabbed me and placed me in a seat right behind him, between Freeman Gosden [radio comedian] and Charlie Farrell [silent film actor]. When the rest scrambled aboard, off we took. I not only got to pull the whistle, but Walt actually let me take his place as engineer—a real sacrifice, since he loves running that train almost more than anything."

In the earliest discussions for Disneyland, there was Walt's constant: "It will be surrounded by a train."

"Walt, you see, he had hunches and he had . . . unusually infallible taste even though he wasn't a sophisticated person. He was a Missouri farm boy, but whatever he liked, he could pretty well know the public would like it, too. And that's why Disneyland is there."

—HERB RYMAN

Walt standing on the railroad station steps, looking out to the vista of Town Square; Main Street, U.S.A.; and Sleeping Beauty Castle, circa 1956.

Overview of Town Square, July 1955. "Bill, people aren't soldiers!" Walt instructed Imagineer Bill Martin. "They don't turn in at sharp angles! Curve the sidewalks! Make the corners round!"

Marvin Davis adds, "It was Walt's idea to have the steam trains circle the whole park so people could get a concept of where things were by taking a train ride."

Or, as Walt said, "to encircle Disneyland and to preview what's inside the land so when guests go by train, they get an idea of 'Oh, let's go in that land and have fun.'"

Walt fell in love with trains as a boy in Marceline, Missouri, where he marveled at the massive steam engines at the depot across from E. P. Ripley Park. Walt recounted, "One day in 1909, when I was eight or nine years old and full of nerve, my buddies dared me to climb into the cab of one of them that stood there, temporarily deserted, and pull the whistle cord. I did so, but as soon as the whistle shrieked, I quickly climbed down and ran like the dickens."

Walt had bragging rights that his uncle Mike was an engineer on the Santa Fe railroad. So did his brother Roy: "I recall how Walt and I would snuggle together in bed and hear the haunting whistle of a locomotive passing in the night. Our uncle Mike was an engineer and he'd blow his whistle—one long and two short—just for us." During the daytime, whenever Walt heard that special toot, he ran across the street from his house and hopped in the slow-moving cab to ride the rest of the way to the Marceline depot. Walt said proudly, "If you can't be an engineer yourself, the next best thing is to have a relative who is one." (Little did he know that one day he'd have his own railroad.)

Later, as a fifteen-year-old, Walt went on to get a job with the Van Noyes Interstate News Company as a a news butcher selling newspapers, cigars, and snacks on the Santa Fe train route from Kansas City and half a dozen states. As an adult, he commuted by train from Los Angeles to New York. Lilly lamented, "It got to be embarrassing when the train would stop in Marceline. Walt would go through the cars, announcing, 'That's my hometown, that's my hometown.'"

After he had achieved success, Walt built what Roy referred to as his brother's "only extravagance," a hobby one-eighth-scale train at his home in Los Angeles. He named it the *Carolwood-Pacific Railroad,* for the street on which his house was located.

Walt retired his home railroad: "It was a lot of fun, but it got so everyone else was riding around in the train, enjoying themselves, while I was wearing myself out stoking coal all day. I finally packed the thing up and shipped it to Disneyland."

Walt continued, "I'm going to get it repainted and displayed in a glass case at the Disneyland and Santa Fe station. That's only right, since it spawned the busy little railroad here in Disneyland and somehow is tied up emotionally with my boyhood experience as a news butcher. Yes, in one way or another I have always loved trains."

TOUR GARDENS

Early on, Tour Guides were introduced to be Walt's representatives in the Magic Kingdom.

Cicely Rigdon started as a ticket seller in 1957 before joining the Guest Relations Department in 1959. She shares, "Walt really liked the Tour Guides. Every time he would come to the park he would always stop by and see us and talk to us. Walt was just a very decent, very nice man. And I believe that is reflected in all of us here at Disneyland, and that this place for family and fun and decency is what it's all about."

The Tour Guides' early costumes eventually settled on an equestrian style; that might be because Walt enjoyed the horse races. He quipped, "This is a Tour Guide costume, sort of a jockey-like costume with a riding crop. And sometimes [Tour Guides] are referred to as Guest Jockeys."

DISNEYLAND CITY HALL (1955)

City Hall is situated right near the entrance, part of Walt's master plan to provide VIP service to his guests from their first steps into the park. Offering everything from maps to advice to "lost person retrieval," this is the epicenter of Guest Relations at Disneyland.

Imagineer Harper Goff explains that the design was partially inspired by his boyhood town: "When I started working on Main Street, I had photographs of Fort Collins [Colorado] taken. I showed them to Walt and he liked them very much.

Imagineer Rolly Crump recalls a story from this location: "Emile Kuri told me that he and Walt used to sit on the steps of City Hall and have sandwiches. He said he was having lunch there on the steps with Walt and all of a sudden nuns came in with all these kids attached to 'em. Walt got up and went over to the head nun and said, 'What is this?' She explained that they tied them to together so they wouldn't run around Disneyland and that they were underprivileged children. 'And so how much did you pay to get in?' Walt asked. She told him and he went over to the booth and got the exact amount of money that they paid and returned it."

Walt sitting on a bench in front of City Hall, 1966.

DISNEYLAND FIREHOUSE (1955)

Almost every small town in America has a firehouse, and Walt's American town is no exception. While it's not a working station, it has an authentic turn-of-the-century design. The fire wagon, on display now, operated between 1955 and 1960. The horses Jess and Bess pulled the wagon; their ceremonial stalls remain in the firehouse, along with their tack.

WALT'S APARTMENT (1955)

"Disneyland was being built while Dad was in the middle of production on *Lady and the Tramp*," Walt's daughter Diane Disney Miller explains. "He'd spend the morning in the studio, then out in Anaheim in the afternoons. And back. It was a long drive. I think he always envisioned he'd have to be there. That he'd want to be there."

Indeed Walt wanted to be there, visiting often on the weekends. He said, "My wife and I have an apartment over the firehouse; it's furnished in the Gay Nineties manner—that's how I keep her interested. When we come out, she sits in the apartment and reads, and I go out and study the place."

The one-room, one-bath apartment was in keeping with the Main Street, U.S.A. theme. Diane elaborates: "Mother and Dad loved the Victorian period. It was the period that they grew up in. But our home was not of that style. This was their little Victorian masterpiece.

"When Dad would travel, they'd go into little antique shops and that's where he acquired some of his miniature collection and bric-a-brac—you know, little china teacups and things. Mother collected cranberry glass. And cranberry is the color that dominates the apartment. It was this little microcosm of the Victorian world. In cranberry red. It was gorgeous."

Walt and Lilly in their Disneyland apartment with grandchildren, 1963.

Interior of the apartment featuring the Edison phonograph.

Diane describes the Disneyland residence in detail: "Near the front door, as you walked in, you'd see this beautiful Edison phonograph with a beautiful green morning glory–shaped horn. Actually, it had morning glories painted around it. And it had a little back cylinder. So we had music up there. Nostalgic music."

The tiny galley had a refrigerator, a grilled-cheese press, a toaster, an ice bucket, an ice crusher (for Walt's favorite cocktail—Scotch mist), and a Tom and Jerry serving set. The bar was stocked with Black & White scotch (Walt's preferred brand), Miller High Life beer, Coca-Cola, 7UP, and V8 juice. Snacks on hand were a smorgasbord of peanuts and assorted mixed nuts from Main Street, U.S.A.'s Candy Palace.

The sitting area had a television, chairs, and two couches that did double duty as foldout beds.

"It was their refuge; it was their little place. The decor, it was all little things that they picked up when they were traveling around the country various times, and it was decorated by Emile Kuri . . . and it was lovingly done. It was really a very cozy family place," Diane continues. "They say that in the morning the park reminds them of a small town waking up.

"Very private. It was for them. It was their residence there, and they would invite people up. If there were special people in the park, Mother and Dad would go out and they would invite them up. Early—it was during *Davy Crockett*—I remember there was some event there that day and Fess Parker and Buddy Ebsen were both out there for it, and Dad was looking out that window and saw them and he said, 'Hey, come on up!'

"He told them how to get around, back behind, and get up to the apartment, and there was a fire pole in it. It's not there now, but there was a door into the closet area that had a fire pole, like the firemen would have, and he showed it to them and said, 'Why don't you guys slide down that?' And they did!"

While it was historically accurate—and fun—Walt had the fire pole removed when kids started shinnying up it to get inside the apartment.

Walt welcomed many guests to his Disneyland home (via stairs, accessible only by going backstage). Twelve-year-old Mouseketeer Sharon Baird was with Walt in his apartment when Disneyland debuted to the world. She remembers: "On the opening day of

"Walt cared about everyone. He would come out of his apartment
at night just to interact with the maintenance crew, with the guys
sweeping the dust out of the trolley tracks on Main Street."

—RON MILLER

Disneyland, we Mouseketeers were in Walt Disney's apartment above the Main Street
fire station when the gates of the park opened for the first time. I was standing next to
him at the window, watching his guests come pouring through the gate. When I looked
at him, he had his hands behind his back, a grin from ear to ear, and I could see a lump
in his throat and a tear streaming down his cheek."

Herb Ryman talks about a time in Walt's apartment when Walt parted the lace curtains
to see the guests entering the park: "See here, they're coming now, they're coming in now!"
he exclaimed. Herb added, "He'd watch them like a kid, because he was just like a little
kid, he just loved everything . . ."

That window might have been one of Walt's favorite vantage points in the park. Diane
recalls, "He could watch the Disneyland parade at the end of the day, and he always got
very emotional when he saw them lower the flag in his Disneyland."

The curtains remain parted—and the lamp lit—a tradition that reminds us Walt's spirit
is always in Disneyland.

William "Sully" Sullivan, who started as a Jungle Cruise skipper in 1955 and went on
to become operations supervisor at Disneyland, recalls, "When I was working graveyard
security, I got this call over the radio from a new employee, who said, 'There's a guy out
here that thinks he's Walt Disney.' It was one o'clock in the morning. So I got on my bike
and I went there and sure as hell it was Walt. He says, 'Thank God, Sully, it's you! This guy
is going to lock me up!' I explained things and walked Walt back to his apartment over the
firehouse and said good night."

FLAGPOLE (1955)

Disneyland was close to completion and there still wasn't a base for the sixty-five-foot-
tall flagpole in Town Square. Since there was a flag retreat planned for Opening Day,
this was a vital detail. Emile Kuri found the perfect one when he passed a car that had
collided with a streetlight in Los Angeles. The downed light had a beautiful base. Emile
was able to purchase it and had it installed in time for Opening Day. It remains Town
Square's stalwart symbol.

FLAG RETREAT CELEBRATION (1955)

"He'd watch the flag lowering at Disneyland every evening they were down there and
tears would flow down his cheeks."

—Diane Disney Miller

The lowering of the American flag every afternoon is a tradition dating back to Abraham
Lincoln's presidency. Walt implemented this sacred ceremony at Disneyland beginning
on Opening Day. He was a fierce patriot and his park would be bipartisan by design: "At
Disneyland, we are not Republican or Democrat—we are representing our country. I've
had Truman, Kennedy, Eisenhower at Disneyland. It's all for the people."

Every evening, veterans visiting Disneyland are acknowledged:

*"To all of you that have served our great nation, on behalf of the Disneyland Resort, we thank you for
your honorable service to America."*

BANK OF AMERICA (1955)/DISNEY GALLERY (2009)

The first bank on Town Square was Bank of America. It was a working branch with tellers handling transactions, which even included souvenir money orders. While they had helped to finance the construction of Disneyland, this institution was likely selected because they had been willing to take a gamble backing *Snow White and the Seven Dwarfs*. Walt and Roy's first full-length animated feature premiered at the Carthay Circle Theatre on December 21, 1937, to critical acclaim. Perhaps Walt paid back the loan (and leap of faith) to Bank of America by offering prime real estate at his other risky venture—Disneyland.

OPERA HOUSE (1955)

The first building finished at Disneyland may have been inspired by Walt's memories of Cater's Opera House in Marceline; it was there he spent his precious pennies to see shows, including a live stage performance of *Peter Pan*. Disneyland's Opera House served a different function before it became an attraction. Admiral Joe Fowler—supervisor of construction—determined that a mill was needed on-site in order for the park to be ready for Opening Day and utilized the Opera House for this purpose in 1954 and early 1955. It is believed that Walt, a fine woodworker himself, pitched in when needed there. His daughter Diane says, "I think he was quite good at [woodworking]. He spent a lot of time doing that . . . Maybe it had something to do with his wanting to be a carpenter. He had great respect for people who could do things with their hands. And I think Daddy himself was skilled."

As you enter the lobby, the park bench on display is one (of three originals) that Walt sat on in Griffith Park, Los Angeles, while he was dreaming about Disneyland: "The idea for Disneyland came about when my daughters were very young and Saturday was always Daddy's day . . .

Walt and Imagineer Vic Greene review the Great Moments with Mr. Lincoln model for Disneyland, July 1965.

I'd take them to the merry-go-round . . . and as I'd sit while they rode the merry-go-round and did all these things—sit on a bench, you know, eating peanuts—I felt that there should be something built where the parents and the children could have fun together. So that's how Disneyland started."

Around the corner, also not to be missed, is an original scale model of Disneyland—exactly as it looked on Opening Day, July 17, 1955.

GREAT MOMENTS WITH MR. LINCOLN (1965)

"It was like working on the first automobile or the first airplane or whatever, and you didn't know whether it would fly or not."

—Marc Davis

Walt had a lifelong affinity for Abraham Lincoln. In the fifth grade, he made his own stovepipe hat and memorized the Gettysburg Address. His performance was so good he was asked to give encores in other classes. When he moved from Marceline to Kansas City, Walt continued to portray the sixteenth president in amateur theatricals for five more years, saying, "I was the best five-foot-six Lincoln that ever trod the boards."

Walt immortalized Lincoln with the Great Moments show, debuted at the 1964–1965 New York World's Fair, then permanently installed at Disneyland in the Opera House.

Mr. Lincoln was the first human Audio-Animatronics figure. Walt had been mulling the idea of Audio-Animatronics characters since the mid-1940s. Years later he explained his concept to his Imagineers. Harriet Burns recollected, "In the shop, we had an early version for the head of Lincoln. I recall several of us were sitting around the plywood table discussing it. There was John Hench, Dick Irvine, Fred [Joerger], and myself. Walt said, 'Hmmm . . . we can call it . . . anima . . . anima . . . animatronics! We can combine

While this photo is often considered to be Walt dressed as Abe Lincoln, it's actually Walt (right) with his pal Walt Pfeiffer (left), dressed for vaudeville, circa 1911. The boys had an act called "The Two Walts," which they performed in local theaters.

"electronics" and "animation"! It will be called animatronics. . . .' And everybody was mumbling all these words together. Then Vic Greene said, 'Yes, but there's sound in there, too.' Walt said, 'Well, that would be "audio" . . .' And so they added the word 'audio' to 'animatronics.' . . . Then Walt said, 'And we can have Lincoln be our first audio-animatronic character!'"

Walt was very involved with every aspect of Lincoln's development: "We were fortunate in being able to secure a life mask that was made of him, and it gave us a chance to know the contours of his face and all of that," Walt continued. "And then by research, we found all of his mannerisms, we selected a voice that fit the closest to what was described as Lincoln's voice—and also how when he started his speech, he'd start it rather high. Then, as he got into his speech, he would come down and modulate his voice more carefully. He was a fellow who could get rather emotional in a speech, too. So we've done everything we can do to create the most lifelike image of Mr. Lincoln. More so than I think any actor could do." Walt concluded, "The final result is so lifelike you may find it hard to believe."

Imagineer Roger Broggie adds that when Walt didn't like Lincoln's gestures during run-through testing, he got up on the stage beside the sixteenth president and said, "You don't move your arms like this. You move 'em like this and you do this and that."

Walt further challenged his Imagineers: "If Lincoln tugged at his lapels, how would he do it?" and "Lincoln always had a long beat on the last syllable of his sentences."

Naturally, Walt was very involved with the script, too, detailing, "We didn't present the Gettysburg Address here in any form for the simple reason, I mean, everybody hears it everywhere. And I think a lot of people think that's the only thing that Lincoln ever said, and I think a lot of people even think that it was written by a fellow by the name of Gettysburg." Instead, Walt used excerpts from Lincoln's speeches delivered in Edwardsville and Springfield, Illinois; Baltimore; and New York City. (Since Walt's passing, the attraction's script has been changed.)

"He's going to be very lifelike and very, very believable," said Walt. "And we've . . . we're finding some wonderful words of Mr. Lincoln that are still prophetic today. And I think it's going to be a *great moment* for the public when they get to sit and hear Mr. Lincoln talk about some of the things . . . what is liberty? You know. The rights and the obligations that we have and all of that. I think it is needed today, too."

Walt felt that Great Moments with Mr. Lincoln "is a different and exciting way to stress history's significance to each of us." And although separate admission was required when it debuted at Disneyland, Walt made a significant exception:

"So that young people may become better acquainted with one of the greatest figures in American history, all Disneyland visitors seventeen years of age or younger are invited to be Walt Disney's guests to spend a few Great Moments with Mr. Lincoln.

A complimentary admission is included with your main entrance ticket."

The exhibits in the lobby include a significant piece personally purchased by Walt. The sixteen-foot replica of the Capitol Building in Washington, D.C., was carved from a single piece of Caen stone. "It has taken me three and a half years to complete my model, but I have enjoyed every minute of it, and feel that many thousands of people who have perhaps never visited the Capitol will look with interest and pleasure at this work," said artist George Lloyd.

Herb Ryman recalls, "It was on exhibit at Robinson's Department Store [in Los Angeles] . . . it was beautifully done. The man [Lloyd] resembled Walt's father. Walt met him and liked him. He said, 'I am going to buy that.'"

Lloyd might have been unaware of his resemblance to Walt's father, Elias; however, he seemed pleased with the purchase and its permanent home at Disneyland: "I sold it to a well-known motion picture man named Walt Disney and it will be on permanent display at his wonderful exhibition ground at Los Angeles."

DISNEYLAND'S VEHICLES
Omnibus (1956)

These double-deckers were inspired by the tour buses of Los Angeles in the twenties and the open-air vehicles at Travel Town in Griffith Park. Imagineer Bob Gurr, who says, "If it moves on wheels at Disneyland, I probably designed it," remembers that when Walt

Walt and his guest King Mohammad of Morocco ride the Omnibus, 1957.

made the decision to add this attraction a year after Disneyland opened, it happened within one hour: "Sometimes he'd just come down to somebody's office room and sit there. He wouldn't say anything, just sit there. One time I spotted that eyebrow go up and he said, 'Bobby, do you know what we haven't got? We haven't got an omnibus on Main Street in Disneyland. I've got a toy in my office. I'll be right back.' When he came back, he gave me the toy as a reference."

Horseless Carriages (1956)
When it was decided that Main Street, U.S.A. needed more antique vehicles, Bob Gurr recalls, "we went out to a place in San Bernardino where there was a crazy old guy in a black suit . . . and he had maybe one hundred fifty old cars, all kinds, a lot of them in very poor condition. He was trying to make a deal with Walt that he would sell him some of those cars and the studio would find somebody to overhaul them and then use them as ride vehicles." In the end, Bob was able to save Walt the hassle (and expense), buying the parts and building the cars himself.

Horse-Drawn Streetcars (1955)
Considering Walt's lifelong love of horses—he rode recreationally and played polo—it was natural for era-appropriate horse-drawn carriages to have a presence on Main Street, U.S.A. Regarding the short walking distance to Sleeping Beauty Castle, Walt mused about his streetcar, "It's not far away, but let's have some fun getting there."

Fire Engine (1958)
A few years after Disneyland opened, Bob Gurr pointed out to Walt that he had a fire station but no fire engine. Walt's response was "You're right, Bobby," and a few hours later the purchase order was approved. (Walt had to request purchase orders, just like everyone else.) Bob designed the 1916-style replica and it became one of Walt's favorite vehicles; he delighted in driving it all over his park before it opened to the public. In August 1966, it was a featured prop in one of the last photographs taken of Walt at Disneyland. He was behind the wheel, grinning ear to ear, with Mickey Mouse riding shotgun.

CANDLELIGHT CEREMONY AND PROCESSIONAL
This beloved Christmastime tradition began at Disneyland in 1958, with sixteen choirs parading down Main Street, U.S.A. to Sleeping Beauty Castle, where they performed with the Dickens Carolers. In 1960, the pageantry, including a full orchestra and celebrity narrators reciting the biblical Christmas story, moved to Town Square. Also that year was the debut of the living Christmas tree, a tiered stage on which the choir performed hymns, along with those on the train station's steps. Walt and his family retreated to his apartment following the ceremony.

Walt pointing at Disneyland Fire Department Wagon No 1.

TOP: *The choir walks along the hub toward Sleeping Beauty Castle, 1958.* **MIDDLE:** *Walt and Lilly wave to the crowds. Dick Van Dyke and family are seated to the right of Walt. December 1965.* **BOTTOM:** *The choir assembled on the steps of the Santa Fe and Disneyland Railroad station, 1956.*

WALT AND TRASH

Walt was a stickler about trash and he helped to popularize the cans with the swinging doors so that guests wouldn't have to lift a lid and see the garbage inside. Later, the trash cans were themed to blend seamlessly into each land. Hot dogs figure into the park's sanitation concerns, too. Walt reportedly paced off the distance between trash cans based on how long it took him to eat a hot dog; he wanted to be sure there would be no reason to drop wrappers on the ground.

The disposal of garbage was one of the myriad details Walt personally attended to. Chuck Boyajian, the first manager of Custodial Relations, was assigned by Walt to go to a "top-notch" hotel and sit in the lobby for a weekend. His task was to observe how a first-class operation handled garbage, making the effort as invisible to guests as possible.

Walt was determined to keep Disneyland spotless, partly to satisfy Lilly: "When I started on Disneyland, my wife used to say, 'But why do you want to build an amusement park? They're so dirty.' I told her that was just the point—mine wouldn't be." Walt kept that promise and could be seen in the park picking up trash himself. "Yep. That was him," said Imagineer Orlando Ferrante. Son-in-law Ron Miller adds, "He was always setting an example for everyone else."

Themed garbage cans for Adventureland (bottom) and Carnation (top).

CHAPTER FIVE
MAIN STREET, U.S.A.

"Many of us fondly remember our 'small hometown' and its friendly way of life at the turn of the century. To me, this era represents an important part of our heritage and thus we have endeavored to recapture those years on Main Street, U.S.A. at Disneyland."

—WALT

Main Street, U.S.A. is both a gateway to the Magic Kingdom and a land unto itself. It's fashioned partly after Walt's boyhood town of Marceline, Missouri, and its thoroughfare Kansas Avenue—both very dear to Walt's heart. He oft repeated, "More things of importance have happened to me in Marceline than have happened since . . . or are likely to in the future." There were other influences; however, ultimately it was designed to represent any small town in America at the turn of the twentieth century.

Walt added his whimsy to Main Street, U.S.A.'s architecture: "It's not apparent at casual glance, but this street is only a scale model. We had every brick and shingle and gas lamp made to scale. This cost more, but it made the street a toy, and the imagination can play more freely with a toy."

"Walt spent weeks and weeks and weeks just laying out curbing to curbing," Herb Ryman recounts. "I said, 'What are you doing?' and he said, 'Well, it's very important that Main Street isn't too big and it can't be too small, because if it's too wide and nobody's in the park and people come in and they'll think there's nobody there; it'll be empty. On the other hand, if it's not wide enough, when there's a crowd there, it'll be too congested, and we don't want that. . . .'"

Among Walt's many delights at Disneyland was that he could "jaywalk" on his Main Street, U.S.A.

West Side
EMPORIUM (1955)
This is another building that draws inspiration from Walt's childhood in Marceline: Murray's Department Store, where Walt's mother, Flora, took him to buy his first pair of overalls. The emotional meaning for Walt was profound; he was no longer a Chicago boy—he was a country boy!

Walt and his authentic ice cream truck, 1955. Designed by Bob Gurr, it was built for Carnation at Disneyland. Walt had one objection, though: the plaque behind the driver's seat read "Carnation." Walt knew that hundreds of pictures a day would be taken inside the truck, so he had the sign replaced with one that said "Disneyland." It was a favorite photo spot for years.

> **"I know more adults who have the children's approach to life. They're people who don't give a hang what the Joneses do. You see them at Disneyland every time you go there. They are not afraid to be delighted with simple pleasures, and they have a degree of contentment with what life has brought—sometimes it isn't much, either."**
>
> —WALT

The Emporium and all the other businesses along the town thoroughfare have something in common that is not authentic to the period—which Walt would normally not approve: the storefront windows were built lower to the ground so little children could peer inside without having to be lifted by an adult.

"Often he squatted down and commented, 'Can you see little kids looking up at this?'" noted biographer Bob Thomas. "Most of his planners had never considered looking at the park from the vantage point of a child."

In Walt's day, the Emporium displayed signs intended to ease the minds of harried parents: "Relax. We do *not* charge for accidental breakage."

It was also near here that Disneyland's first president, Jack Lindquist, observed on Christmas Eve, 1955: "A family caught my attention, and as the mother, father, their ten-year-old son and younger daughter walked down Main Street, I followed them. They all held hands. They talked to each other and appeared to be a close-knit family. When they arrived at the Christmas tree in Town Square, next to the Emporium with the mechanical Santa Claus and dolls in the window, the little girl tugged on her mom's arm and said, 'Mom, this really was better than having Santa Claus' . . . So for this family, their time at the park was probably Christmas. The kids would forego toys, and mom and dad wouldn't receive presents. To me, this one brief moment proved to be my most meaningful memory at the park, because it symbolized what we mean to people."

ELIAS DISNEY WINDOW (1955)
Elias was Walt's father. It is believed that the 1895 date on the window reflects the year Elias began working as a contractor in Chicago. It's often repeated that he was stern and demanding; however, Walt never wavered in his love for him: "I had tremendous respect for him. I always did. In spite of his arguments, my dad, I worshiped him . . . nothing but family counted."

MAIN STREET, U.S.A. TRIBUTE WINDOWS
The windows on Main Street, U.S.A. are "screen credits" for the people who helped Walt build Disneyland. Imagineer Harper Goff explains further, "Walt found it necessary to open Disneyland even though many areas were not yet completed. On Main Street, some of the ground floor shops still had interior construction underway after the park was opened to the public. Each night, workmen would go in and do a little bit more to finish the interiors. In the meantime, we would put up a serious-looking sign that might say 'Harper Goff will be opening his shoe store here soon,' and we'd have some sample shoes in the window . . . but there was nothing inside the store. That was the beginning of the tradition of name signs on the windows."

THE FORTUOSITY SHOP—FORMERLY UPJOHN PHARMACY (1955–1970)
It was a series of serendipities that brought the first lessee to this location at 115 Main Street, U.S.A. Upjohn's director of advertising Jack Gauntlet had heard rumblings about Disneyland in 1953. He thought the park would be the perfect place to market Upjohn—

TOP: *Renié Conley's concept sketch for a cashier costume at the Mad Tea Party attraction.* **BOTTOM:** *Upjohn Pharmacy, 1963. The tribute windows are the one above the entrance and the one to its right.*

> ## "Main Street in Disneyland reminds Dad and Mother of the rural America they knew in the years before World War I."
> ### —DIANE DISNEY MILLER

and its products, like Kaopectate and Cheracol—to the general public. He took his big idea to the top, Managing Director and Chairman of the Board Donald Gilmore. It was a surprisingly easy sell; his boss said something like "Let me call my friend Walt, and we'll make this happen." Unbeknownst to Jack, Donald was Walt's neighbor at Smoke Tree Ranch in Palm Springs. The deal was made. Walt had already been leasing space in Disneyland to businesses to raise capital for its construction; it was a bonus that Gilmore was his pal. (Gilmore has a tribute window above the entrance, along with other Upjohn alumni E. G. Upjohn, Fred Allen, and C. V. Patterson.)

The Victorian theme of Main Street, U.S.A. was the perfect setting for the authentic 1880–1910 apothecary Upjohn planned. However, when they were presented plans for the building, they rejected them—yes, rejected Disney—insisting it would be their design or nothing. Disney conceded, unaware that the art director for Upjohn's *Scope* magazine was world-renowned designer Will Burtin. After visiting old-time apothecaries in New York City, he designed the faithful reproduction at Disneyland.

Upjohn was a popular attraction (there was no retail) with real pharmacists—not cast members—behind the counter. It closed in 1970. The interior, minus the authentic pharmacy props, remains largely the same today.

CARNATION CAFÉ (1955)

Walt sat by himself in the back of this restaurant, observing as anonymously as possible; cast members knew not to approach him here. Sometimes he'd sip a milkshake made by

Walt rides in a parade with matador Carlos Arruza from Mexico City in front and Edmundo Gonzales, Mexico Consul General in Los Angeles riding in back. The occasion was part of a celebration for "Salute to Mexico," presented by People to People International, 1963.

Shirley, who knew how to make them "just right" for the boss, according to chef Oscar Martinez (her husband and the longest-tenured employee at Disneyland). "He liked them runny. A combination of chocolate and vanilla ice cream, with chocolate syrup. He liked them with not too much ice cream and not too much milk," Oscar recalls.

One of Disneyland's first hires, former park supervisor Bob Penfield, recalls a memorable moment outside the Carnation Café: "At the Carnation patio on Main Street, there were some people standing, watching the parade, and Walt was sitting behind them, eating with some guests. One of the park supervisors asked the people standing, 'Could you please move so Walt can see?'

"Walt heard him and said, 'Oh, no. They're paying guests! They're what makes this place go.'"

The tribute window above the restaurant's entrance is in honor of a woman often overlooked by accounts of Disneyland history, costume designer Renié Conley. She was handpicked by Walt, who respected her work in motion pictures. The admiration was mutual. Renié sent this letter to Walt shortly after Disneyland opened:

> Dear Mr. Disney:
>
> May I tell you again what a joy and pleasure it was to be a part of your won-derful project. To design the costumes for Disneyland was an exciting challenge and I enjoyed it, and working with you and your nice associates was a very pleasant experience.
>
> As an artist I believe that I can appreciate more than most the concept of lasting beauty and charm which you have created and I am very proud to have contributed a small part of it.

GIBSON GIRL ICE CREAM PARLOR—
FORMERLY SUNKIST CITRUS HOUSE (1960–1989)

Before this was an ice cream parlor, it was the home of lessee Sunkist. In the wee hours of the morning, before the park opened, Walt used to "break in" to the Citrus House—he didn't own it; Sunkist did—to make orange juice using the modern extractors. (He always paid, by the way, leaving coins on the counter.) Pretty soon it occurred to the shop's man-ager, Bo Foster, to give Walt an electric juicer for his Disneyland apartment. He arranged for Walt's secretary to alert him anytime Walt would be in the park, ensuring there would always be plenty of fresh Sunkist oranges in the galley kitchen. While that was considerate, Walt preferred playing with the machines at Sunkist, explaining, "Bo, the juice just doesn't taste the same. I'd rather have your juice fresh from the spigot!"

Those oranges had more than one use, according to Rolly Crump: "Walt was staying in his apartment and there was jackhammering. He came down to Main Street with a sack of oranges. He sat on the curb and peeled himself an orange. So he's sitting there on the curb at three o'clock in the morning eating oranges and the guys finally realize there's Walt. They went over and said, 'Sorry, did we wake you up? We can come back later.'

Walt with Sunkist Advertising Manager, Russell Z. Eller, 1960.

A "wienie" in Walt-speak is something that attracts attention. Sleeping Beauty Castle is the first wienie in Disneyland, enticing guests toward the hub. Main Street, U.S.A., 1964.

> **"I love to visit there myself. But I'm usually too busy to do anything but watch the crowds, noting what they like best, what needs must be filled, and how the traffic flows. If I want to enjoy myself, I go to Disneyland before it is open and drive around the empty streets like a kid."**
>
> —WALT

"'No,' Walt replied. 'It's more important that you get these tracks ready before the park opens than for me to get any sleep.' Then he offered, 'Do you guys want an orange?'"

PENNY ARCADE (1955)

In the back of the Penny Arcade is Disneyland's Welte orchestrion. Built to simulate an orchestra, this massive instrument has 265 pipes, bass drum, snare drum, timpani, cymbal, and triangle. It plays automatically on a timed schedule and never requires a coin. Manufactured in Germany in 1907, it was purchased by Walt in 1953 and placed here in 1955.

CANDY PALACE (1955)

Part of the magic of the Candy Palace, also known as Candyland, is the scents pumped onto Main Street, U.S.A. In the early days, the candy was prepared off-site and delivered to the park. In the sixties, however, a cooking and prep area was built in the front of the shop with a large window. An innovation then: Guests could see the candy-making

Walt sits casually on the back of the Main Street Horse-Drawn Street Car, 1956. It would have been in keeping with Walt's character to pay the ten-cent fare.

Walt and Roy with Albert Zurcher on Marceline's main street, Kansas Avenue, 1956. The 1899 building stands today and is undergoing a major renovation.

show! This made Walt one of the first in America to have what is now commonplace—an open kitchen.

COCA-COLA REFRESHMENT CORNER (1955)

"Coke Corner" draws inspiration from the iconic Zurcher Building in Walt's hometown of Marceline, Missouri. It had a large Coca-Cola mural painted on the side and a diagonal entrance on the corner, just like the Kansas Avenue building from his boyhood; there's little doubt this was Walt's inspiration.

An example of ingenuity is found above the entrance. When the electricians installed the sockets for the red and white ceiling lights in 1955, they used an odd number. When it was time to screw in the bulbs, they discovered they were one socket short. To keep the red-white pattern going, a low-tech solution was implemented: paint one bulb half red and half white. Or as former attraction host and Disneyland operations supervisor Jim Cora observed, "Yep, that would be just like Walt: 'Paint the thing both colors.'"

THE PAVILION (1955–1963)
Jolly Holiday Bakery Cafe (2015)

This restaurant featured two distinct facades—and entrances—in Walt's era: Victorian on the Main Street, U.S.A. side and Polynesian on the Adventureland side (where the Tahitian Terrace once stood). The Pavilion was leased until Walt decided to operate it himself in 1963. With the many modern changes, the architecture remains essentially the same.

It was here that John Hench observed Walt from afar: "Walt was also keen to make dining a good experience for guests, not just a necessity. He would walk the park in disguise, wearing an old hat and dark glasses, observing how people were treated. On one

Outside the Main Street Cinema, 1961. Walt tells us, "Other people can have their bands, thrill rides, and all this stuff, but we've got the Disney characters, and don't think they aren't important! When you see people come in with their children and one of our characters appears, they run to them and get their cameras."

of these walks, I saw him stop at the newly opened restaurant with table seating outside. A young boy was busing dishes, scraping them into a cardboard box at the table in front of diners—not a very appetizing thing to watch. Walt walked over to the boy, patiently and quietly explained to him that cleaning plates should not be exposed to the guests, and asked the boy to take the used dishes back to the kitchen to clean them. Walt waved his hand a bit; the boy nodded and removed the dishes. I watched the whole thing from a distance. I keep seeing this picture in my mind; I was really shocked by the whole thing. It did look bad from the guests' point of view, but Walt didn't raise hell with the busboy's boss; he spoke only to the boy. I am sure that neither the boy nor the diners knew that it was Walt. It was typical of Walt to go to the source of a problem in this way."

This location was briefly Stouffer's Plaza Pavilion (1962–1963), operated by Vern Stouffer, known for his frozen food and restaurants, with a deal brokered by Joyce Hall, Walt's pal of Hallmark fame. Their long friendship began in 1932 when they first signed a licensing deal to produce greeting cards. (Interestingly, Hallmark did not set up shop on Main Street, U.S.A. until 1960; Gibson Greeting Cards was the original lessee.)

"Disneyland is often called a magic kingdom because it combines fantasy and history, adventure and learning, together with a variety of recreation and fun designed to appeal to everyone."

—WALT

In Hall's book *When You Care Enough*, he explains how three little girls he met on an intercontinental flight expressed his feelings about Walt better than he ever could:

"I asked if they had a good time in London. And one said, 'Yes, but we would have rather gone to California.' Surprised, I wondered why. The oldest girl answered, 'To see Disneyland and Burbank.' And what did they want to see in Burbank? She said, 'Walt Disney.' She knew his studio was there. I asked if they thought Walt Disney was a real man or someone more like Santa Claus. The oldest girl thought this over and carefully answered, 'Both.' And I agreed with her."

East Side
MAIN STREET CINEMA (1955)

Once again, it's apparent this architecture is an homage to Walt's hometown, this time the Uptown Theatre. Built in 1930, it would not have been a childhood memory of Walt's; however, he visited Marceline three times as an adult and filmed his hometown himself in 1946.

Inside the box office the ticket taker's Disneyland badge reads TILLY, MARCELINE. This is likely a pun on "till," an old-fashioned name for a cash register. While it may be just a coincidence, there was a waitress with the same name in Marceline at the time Walt lived there.

In Walt's era, silent pictures played here—"no talkies"—as this was in keeping with the turn-of-the-century theater. Walt wore his heart on his sleeve when it came to movies: "If you can pull a tear out of them, they'll remember your picture. That little piece of pathos was Chaplin's secret. Some directors in Hollywood are embarrassed by sentimentality. As for me, I like a good cry."

The Mickey Mouse shorts that now adorn the screens offer guests the opportunity to see Walt's early animation, including *Plane Crazy*, the very first Mickey Mouse cartoon produced, although it wasn't seen widely until 1929. *Steamboat Willie* is considered the debut of the mouse that started it all.

Walt explains, "Our first sound cartoon at the Disney Studio was *Steamboat Willie*. This was also the first public appearance of Mickey Mouse." The premiere was November 18, 1928. That date is also considered Mickey Mouse's birthday—Minnie's, too!

MARKET HOUSE (1955)

Evoking the feel of yesteryear, Walt envisioned this as a meeting place as much as a mercantile. With all the details he attended to at Disneyland, stocking the shelves of the shops was not high on his list. Bob Thomas explains, "He paid little attention to merchandising but he insisted on two things: all articles must be authentic to the period; and products had to be of good quality."

CENTER STREET (1955)
Water Fountain

This is not just another water fountain. The thirst quencher tucked in the back corner of the courtyard is a serious piece of Disneyland history. It is encased in what was the demonstration wall for the masons while the park was under construction; it was wheeled out to the center of Main Street, U.S.A. as a reference. Notice the patterns of the bricks are far from identical, as they represent the different styles found on the walls and around windows on the thoroughfare.

Hotel Marceline

Although Walt wasn't likely to use an alias in Marceline, one he used when checking into hotels around the world: William Edward James. The *W* in William was for Walt, and the *E* in Edward was for Elias.

Main Street, U.S.A on Opening Day, July 17, 1955.

SWIFT'S RED WAGON INN (1955–1964)
Plaza Inn (1965)
This restaurant was envisioned by Walt to be a place where families could take their time and enjoy a leisurely—and elegant—meal. Walt insisted on fine furnishings for the restaurant, including a custom-made Baccarat chandelier. He knew that even though the eatery was serving meals at reasonable prices, his guests would appreciate the extravagant environment.

As with all buildings at Disneyland, it was authentic to the era, thanks to Walt's purchase of an opulent 1870s mansion located in the posh St. James Park neighborhood of Los Angeles. The home was scheduled to be demolished when Walt dispatched his head decorator, Emile Kuri, to salvage everything useful from the estate. The most dramatic pieces remain, including the stained glass ceiling and leaded cut-glass entrance doors.

By 1965, Walt had taken possession of most of the lessees' restaurants. (When Disneyland opened, Walt did not have the capacity to run "feeding operations," as he referred to them, and thus leased them to outside contractors.) This included Swift's Red Wagon Inn. With its grandeur long lost, Walt embarked on an ambitious remodel of what some consider his favorite Disneyland restaurant. Walt had intended to have "singing birds, canary birds, finches in a beautiful cage, and live plants and things"; however, for health code reasons, the birds never made the show. Empty cages still hang in the atriums in Walt's honor.

Overseen by John Hench (whom Walt sent to UCLA to learn about the business of restaurants), the Victorian splendor was returned and a more modern Disney touch added: the Hidden Mickeys in the scalloped eaves.

HIDEOUT (1955–1964)
From the earliest planning documents to the construction of Disneyland, Walt admonished his cost-cutting staff, "The hideout stays!"

First located behind the Red Wagon Inn's atrium closest to Main Street, the large "Disney Room" offered Walt a private area to entertain. The original triptych windows are still visible across from First Aid.

However, with the Plaza Inn's 1965 remodel, that space was needed for a modern kitchen and employee cafeteria. Walt's hideout moved to a much smaller space behind the other atrium, on the Tomorrowland side. After this downsizing, Walt recognized that more VIP space was needed, not less. That prompted him to start planning Club 33 in New Orleans Square.

Walt's hideout door, with its colorful stained glass accents, remains on the Tomorrowland side of the Plaza Inn, near the restrooms, on the very back of the wraparound porch. A similar stained glass door is in Walt's apartment leading to the balcony.

POPCORN PEOPLE (KNOWN UNOFFICIALLY AS TOASTIE-ROASTIES)
Walt loved popcorn! And he found a way to make it part of the show. There's a tiny

---

"I caught sight of a man far down the street. Alone. Quietly regarding the place he had so long envisaged, now complete, ready to bring pleasure and happy satisfactions to the millions that will visit it. And I was reminded that he, too, was a Main Streeter, never weaned from the common bond with the great majority of American small town and country folk, their taste and ideals, despite identification with big cities as an eminent world figure."

—JACK JUNGMEYER

figure inside each cart that was a feature of the manufacturer dating back to the 1890s. At Disneyland, the characters turning the canisters are themed to the land in which they perform—for instance, a turn-of-the-century clown on Main Street, U.S.A. and a spaceman in Tomorrowland, a nod to the costumed character of Walt's era. Discovering the rest is up to you!

WALT AND WALKING

"Like a kid with a new toy—the biggest, shiniest toy in the world—Walt used to wander through the park, gawking as happily as any tourist."
—Roy O. Disney

"Father does more walking than anyone I know . . . He never seems to sit down. I don't know why he covers so much ground, unless it's because he has a hunger to see in person what's happening at the studio and at the park."
—Diane Disney Miller

"I think that's probably the closest to what was Walt's MO: the walking around."
—Bob Gurr

"Walt would regularly walk through the park, looking for problems or things to improve. He was good at it and always welcomed suggestions. I guess it was due to his days on the farm and delivering papers, because he could cover a lot of distance on foot, without seeming to be in a hurry."
—Van France

"I was so astonished by the way Walt would create a kind of live-action cross-dissolve when passing from one area of Disneyland to another. He would even insist on changing the texture of the pavement at the threshold of each new land because, he said, 'You can get information about a changing environment through the soles of your feet.'"
—John Hench

"He walked fast and expected everyone to keep up."
—Charles Ridgway

"That was the only park that Walt ever walked in, manipulated, moved things around—which he did all the time."
—Marty Sklar

Walt walking around the hub, 1966.

CHAPTER SIX
THE HUB

"To walk from Town Square, down Main Street, and through each of these realms is to travel only a mile and a quarter. But that distance is measured not in steps or in hours; it is measured in personal experiences."

—WALT

W alt knew from studying amusement parks in Europe that people could easily get exhausted from all the walking. When designing Disneyland, he wanted to ensure his guests would be comfortable. He explained to Herb Ryman, "I want to have these radiating spokes from the hub. So that people who are tired, or sick, or old could say, 'Well, you kids go on ahead. We'll meet you here in forty-five minutes.'

"I planned it so each place is right off the hub . . . I don't want sore feet here. They make people tired and irritable. I want 'em to leave here happy. They'll be able to cover the whole place and not travel more than a couple of miles.

"The more I go to other amusement places of the world, the more I am convinced of the wisdom of the original concept of Disneyland. I mean the idea of having a single entrance through which all the traffic would flow, then a hub off which the various areas were situated. That gives people a sense of orientation: they know where they are at all times. And it sure saves a lot of walking."

SLEEPING BEAUTY CASTLE

Initially referred to as a medieval castle and the Fantasyland Castle, and at one point planned to be called Snow White's Castle in honor of Walt's original feature film princess, Walt eventually settled on Sleeping Beauty Castle to promote his upcoming film, which premiered more than three years after Disneyland opened.

There was another original idea that changed at Walt's whim: the front of the castle.

In a meeting with fellow designers, Herb Ryman was concerned that the front of the castle looked too much like its inspiration—Neuschwanstein castle in Bavaria. "I picked it up and moved the obvious Neuschwanstein part that was facing Main Street and turned it around to the Fantasyland side," Herb elaborates. "At that moment Walt Disney was standing behind us in the door and looked at this castle and the way I'd turned it around. And he had his hands on his hips and was smiling and he said, 'Well, I like that a lot better.'"

Walt in the newly opened Plaza Inn, 1965. Here with his customary cup of coffee. He drank it black, always. And insisted coffee be ten cents at Disneyland, a price that remained well after he passed away.

Decades later Walt's good friend author Ray Bradbury was visiting Disneyland. On this occasion, he looked up and noticed—for the first time—the spire on the top right of the castle gleaming in gold—a spire he recognized as a replica of the one found on top of Notre-Dame Cathedral in Paris.

He called John Hench at Imagineering: "How long has Viollet-le-Duc's spire been on the side of Sleeping Beauty Castle?"

"Thirty years," said Hench.

"My God. I never noticed it before. Who put it there?"

"Walt," said Hench.

Bradbury remained curious and pressed further: "Why?"

"Because he loved it," replied Hench simply.

PARTNERS STATUE

It wasn't until many years after Walt passed that the *Partners* statue was conceived. Imagineer Blaine Gibson was called out of retirement to sculpt the 3D tribute to Walt and his mouse. Imagineer Marty Sklar and John Hench assisted in the design. It was unveiled in 1993 in celebration of Mickey Mouse's sixty-fifth birthday.

There are a few specific Walt-centric details to notice:

On Walt's right hand is a claddagh wedding ring, a tribute to his Irish heritage. He and Lilly wore these in addition to their wedding rings on the traditional left ring finger.

Walt's tie has the STR brand. *STR* stands for Smoke Tree Ranch, the Palm Springs enclave where Walt had a desert home. Smoke Tree was very special to Walt; it was close to Los Angeles yet far removed from the Hollywood scene. The casual community and cowboy lifestyle appealed to Walt's simple ways, and it was likely the one place in the world he could be a regular guy. (Walt sold his first home at Smoke Tree Ranch to help finance Disneyland. He also offered his fellow residents an investment opportunity in Disneyland; few invested, and many of those who didn't regretted it.)

"The *Partners* statues in the parks were done by sculptor Blaine Gibson, who is absolutely phenomenal about that kind of thing," reminiscences Disneyland operations supervisor Sully. "His interpretation of Walt on that statue is probably the closest anyone could get, but it still doesn't really capture the boss, because he was always so animated. He wasn't ever still."

Blaine remarked of his masterpiece, "That wasn't my hands that did it; it was my heart."

Surrounding Walt are his good friends Goofy, Pluto, Dumbo, Pinocchio, Minnie Mouse, Donald Duck, Chip and Dale, and the White Rabbit.

Walt's immortal words are emblazoned on the plaque below his and Mickey's feet:

"I think what I want Disneyland to be most of all is a happy place where parents and children can have fun together."

A KISS GOODNIGHT

Walt loved fireworks ever since he was a young boy in Marceline; his hometown put on fireworks displays every Fourth of July, which is why Disneyland has a nightly spectacular behind Sleeping Beauty Castle. He called the tradition "a kiss goodnight"—his way of thanking guests for coming to his park.

TOP: *Lilly, Diane, Walt, and Sharon in front of Notre-Dame Cathedral, 1951. The chapel spire has been on Sleeping Beauty Castle since Opening Day; however, it was a pale color (possibly wooden) then. It was repainted gold in the early sixties.* **BOTTOM:** *Perpetually forward-thinking, Walt is shown pointing toward the future. Always a team, Walt and Mickey Mouse.*

TOP: *Walt at Swift's Red Wagon Inn, 1962 (pages 59 and 62). As was his practice, he waited in line for his food, just as he waited in line to ride the attractions. With Joe Fowler and representatives of Stouffer's.* **MIDDLE:** *The entrance to the second Hideout on the Tomorrowland side of the Plaza Inn (page 62).* **BOTTOM:** *Walt conducting a meeting in the original "Disney Room" (page 62), 1957.*

> **"Enthusiasm and optimism together. He was enthusiastic about everything. He never thought anything would turn out badly."**
> —LILLY DISNEY

Songwriter Richard Sherman and his wife ran into Walt one evening on their way out of the park. "Walt, we just had to thank you for the most wonderful time today," commented Richard. "In fact, when the fireworks started and the music was playing and Tinker Bell flew across the sky, I was so overcome with happy emotions that I was crying. Walt looked me straight in the eye and with a little smile said, 'You know, I do that every time. . . . Now drive home carefully.' With a fond wink, Walt headed for his apartment above the fire station."

Walt and the beaver inspired by his True-Life Adventures film Beaver Valley *(1950). The same beaver is also a character in the* Mine Train Through Nature's Wonderland *attraction (1960–1977). The STR logo for Smoke Tree Ranch (page 66) is clearly visible on his tie, 1960.*

DISNEYLANDSCAPES

"Walt said, 'I went in the [Jungle Cruise] river ride and saw a bunch of little buckets along the bank with little saplings about this high in there. I want trees in there!' Walt wanted real trees, and there were only a few orange trees in there from the original orchards. We had used some of them, turned upside down, to look like mangrove roots. I found I could buy medium-size trees and bring them in . . . So Bill Evans and I found some trees there in Anaheim, and around Orange County, and then we took off in this Buick, looking for trees. We drove all around in places like Pasadena, seeing great big nice trees. We'd go up to people and ask them: 'Any chance that you're tired of that tree? We'll give you two hundred dollars and carry it away.' Most of these people just looked at us like it was some kind of joke. We went to Beverly Hills because someone told Bill Evans about a great big banyan tree somebody had up there. When we got there I said: 'God, that's just what we need.' We didn't really want to talk to the guy who had nurtured such a beautiful tree . . . but I went up there and rang the bell. When the guy came out, I said: 'This may sound funny to you, but I'm doing a thing for Disneyland and I need a tree like this. I wonder if there is any chance in the world that you'd sell that tree?' And he said: 'That big old tree there? I'm so tired of that thing.' We got that tree for just the work to remove it and a small replacement tree we put in for him . . . We put it in the back of the ride, by the hippos."
—Harper Goff

"Yesterday it was a peaceful 160 acres of orange groves; today fantastic castles and rocket ships and part of the old West itself are rising in front of your eyes. Despite all the construction, it was the planting that awed me. Walt bought $400,000 worth of trees and shrubs; he depleted our nurseries and is now importing trees from Santa Barbara and San Diego. One hill is completely covered with pines. . . . Cactus from Arizona already dots Disney's painted desert. . . ."
—Hedda Hopper

"Walt wanted each tree to fit its location—maples, sycamores, and birches for the Rivers of America; pines and oaks for Frontierland, et cetera. He sometimes rejected a tree with the comment 'It's out of character.'"
—Bill Evans

"Walt Disney wanted a 'green' park, everything evergreen, for he recalled the cold winters of his childhood when he used to look up at the bare branches of the trees and shiver. Disneyland must be Eternal Spring."
—Ruth Patricia Shellhorn

"Chlorophyll Characters. Walt saw topiary in the gardens of European nobility, however he was intrigued to take it beyond the fuss of stylized hedges and geometrical shapes—he wanted to recreate his characters out of greenery for Disneyland."
—Vacationland Fall/Winter 1982/83

"I remember when we opened, if anybody recalls, we didn't have enough money to finish the landscaping. And I had Bill Evans go out and put Latin tags on all the weeds."
—Walt

"Disneyland was a huge success because he was down there every day with his boots and straw hat and telling people to move this plant more to the right and this tree to the left so the people standing here could see the steamboat coming around the bend. Nothing escaped his eye."
—Ward Kimball

"At Disneyland a jungle must have a jungle landscape. The Rivers of America must be banked by trees which are indigenous to American rivers . . . To achieve the right effect, our Disneyland landscape architects combined their talents with those of builders and maintenance personnel and created a believable and authentic scenes of nature's own design."
—Walt

"It was a miracle Disneyland ever got open on time. Those last few days were frantic. I saw gardeners spraying grass, bushes and flowers with green paint instead of water, because the plants had died."
—Art Linkletter

"Not only can I add things, but even the trees will keep growing. The thing will get more beautiful every year."
—Walt

"In the year before Disneyland opened, you just couldn't escape Walt. He toured the place daily. After I finished planting a pepper tree beside the Plaza Pavilion Restaurant, Walt walked by and made a comment in passing that it was a little too close to the curb. So I moved all ten tons of it a little ways back. The next day he walked by and didn't say a word. He just smiled."
—Bill Evans

"Below the station, on the bank facing the parking lot, is a floral picture of 'Mickey Mouse,' symbol of Walt Disney's famous career. Even this little part of the project took much thought, and many designs were made before the final selection."
—Ruth Patricia Shellhorn

DISNEYLAND, INC.

INTER-OFFICE COMMUNICATION
10-02A 5M 6-55 ⊛

Date July 11, 1955

To Jack Evans   From Joe Fowler

Subject _____

When are you going to plant Mickey Mouse in the entrance? Looks to me like the time is getting pretty late.

JF:es

With less than a week before opening, Admiral Joe Fowler, in charge of Disneyland's construction, sent a memo to landscape designer Jack Evans, brother and partner of Bill Evans (who passed away in 1958), asking when the Mickey Mouse floral portrait will be planted.

CHAPTER SEVEN
ADVENTURELAND

"Everyone has a dream of traveling to mysterious far-off places, or exotic tropical regions of the world. To create a land which would make these dreams a reality, we pictured ourselves far from civilization, in the remote jungles of Asia and Africa. The result is Adventureland."

—WALT

WALT DISNEY'S ENCHANTED TIKI ROOM (1963)

Notably, this is the only attraction at Disneyland with Walt Disney's name on it, and it's his first attraction with Audio-Animatronics figures.

Harriet Burns recalled Walt's vision: "He said, 'We can have lots of birds—and some of them will flip their wings and tails, and some of them will turn their heads and tweet. But they'll all breathe.'

"And I thought, 'Breathe? You know this is not going to be an easy project!'"

Interestingly, it was Harriet (with a little unknowing help from Walt) who helped make that magic happen. A material that could stretch with each bird's breath was needed. The Imagineers were stumped. Harriet discovered a solution while watching her boss; the fabric covering his elbow stretched when bent and didn't bunch when straightened. She observed, "So Walt had this blue sweater that had baggy sleeves; he loved that blue sweater. So he was in talking to us, with that sweater going all the time with his elbows—because he acted everything up. And I looked at his elbows, and I thought, 'You know—that works great! It's brushed wool, and his elbows keep moving, and it looks good.'" Harriet added real feathers to complete the lifelike effect.

Before there was a permanent installation in Adventureland, there was a mock-up at the studio. Walt invited in-house songwriters Richard and Robert Sherman to see the singing birds and help solve a nagging problem.

"After it was over, we said, 'It's wonderful,'" Richard recalls. He then asked, "Walt, what is it?"

"That's what you guys are going to write a song about," answered Walt. "It's a great show, but nobody knows what the thing is all about. Any ideas, boys?"

"Well, our reaction was absolute terror. We had to think fast," recalls Richard. "Luckily we remembered that about two years earlier we had written a lengthy calypso to cover a lot of boring footage showing how Disney crews had carted tons and tons of equipment

Walt in one of his "working" hats (page 89).

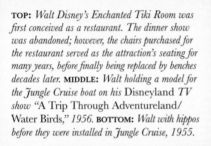

TOP: *Walt Disney's Enchanted Tiki Room was first conceived as a restaurant. The dinner show was abandoned; however, the chairs purchased for the restaurant served as the attraction's seating for many years, before finally being replaced by benches decades later.* **MIDDLE:** *Walt holding a model for the Jungle Cruise boat on his* Disneyland *TV show "A Trip Through Adventureland/ Water Birds," 1956.* **BOTTOM:** *Walt with hippos before they were installed in Jungle Cruise, 1955.*

"I want the skippers to act as if every trip on the Jungle Cruise is their first trip. I want them to act surprised when the hippos suddenly rise out of the water. The skippers need to be as surprised as the guests."

—WALT

to Tobago to film *Swiss Family Robinson* . . . We wrote the lengthy gag-filled calypso Tiki Room song, which performs the all-important task of explaining to the audience what they are about to see and hear."

Initially it was planned as a restaurant (notice the remnants that remain inside the Tiki Room: the banquettes along the walls and the coffee station beneath the Enchanted Fountain), but that idea was tossed when Walt realized it would be too difficult to time the meal to the birds' performance. He abandoned the dinner show, and focused solely on the spectacle overhead.

"This is the latest thing we've done with Audio-Animatronics," Walt said. "It's just animation with sound, run by electronics, Audio-Animatronics."

Walt explained in detail: "It's an extension of animated drawings. We take an inanimate object and make it move. Everything is programmed on tape: the birds' movements, lighting effects, and sounds. We turn on the tape and the bids do their stuff.

"You know, the same scientific equipment that guides rockets to the moon is used to make José and his little friends in the Tiki Room sing, talk, move, and practically think for themselves. I guess you could call him a creature of the space age. They say a bird in the hand is worth two in the bush. But this little fella here is worth a fortune—because we poured a fortune into creating him!

"We operate fifteen hours a day. . . . My tiki bird show goes on three times an hour, and I don't have to stop for coffee breaks and all that kind of stuff, you see."

When Walt was asked if anyone else was doing anything like his Enchanted Tiki Room, he replied, "I don't know anyone crazy enough."

JUNGLE CRUISE (1955)

Walt's brother-in-law and right-hand man, Bill Cottrell, thinks all the way back to 1941 and the Good Neighbor Program trip to South America (during which the Disney group became known as El Grupo, a bellhop's nickname for them), wondering about Walt's first inkling for this attraction: "In one tiny Colombian town, we took a jungle launch thirty miles upstream into the rain forest. I wonder if this wasn't the forerunner of the Jungle Cruise at Disneyland."

Walt was intimately involved with this epic adventure. Blaine Gibson explains what happened at the studio in the planning stages: "Walt came in and saw our model, and I remember he said, 'You know, we need an elephant climbing out on the bank . . . maybe reaching out for some of the branches, like in our nature pictures.' . . . And then he pushed down his pants a little bit so he could get that 'elephant look' and he used his hand for a trunk, and he got up on a chair . . . I actually went ahead and modeled him as that elephant. It's still in Disneyland as far as I know, on the far side of the pool, climbing up the bank."

Imagineer Sam McKim adds more about Walt acting out the roles of the jungle animals: "I had a sketch of a big gorilla coming up out of the grass. Walt said, 'Now, look, this gorilla, you can't see he's down in the grass, see. And he comes up and he looks at the people in the boats . . . and he roars! That'll get them at the end of the ride.'"

Bob Thomas recalls the early days of the attraction's construction: "We got in a Jeep; there was no place to walk. Main Street was blank; there was no castle, just a few orange

Walt and Roy were a solid team, yet it appears Walt had some sibling rivalry fun when it came to the Jungle Cruise. "We're going to have an elephant pool and an African veldt based around the lion kill. Where the lions make a kill – that's where everything else comes," Walt explains. "Zebra will stand and watch brother zebra being eaten." Louis Francuz is standing behind Walt.

"Just listening to him talk was an adventure in itself."
—CHARLIE RIDGWAY

trees. They were digging out Adventureland and we drove into this pit where the jungle boats were going to be and he acted out the whole routine.

"'Giraffes, you can see them in the trees over there and then you come into the hippo pond. Look out! There's a hippo coming right at the boat! And the boat swerves and you get a splash of water . . . And you get into all kinds of hazards—alligators, lions. You go down the rapids until you finally arrive back at civilization.'

"In Walt's mind, the whole trip was in this hole in the ground. I don't think the Imagineers were able to capture the whole experience the way Walt described it. It was unforgettable," Thomas concludes.

Dick Nunis, who held many positions at Disneyland, working his way up to operations manager, had an exacting encounter after the attraction opened: "On one of my first days in Adventureland, I was at the Jungle Cruise when Walt stepped off a boat and asked, 'Dick, what is that trip time?' I told him seven minutes. He said, 'Well, I just got a four-and-a-half-minute trip. How would you feel if you went to a movie and they cut out the center reel? I went through that hippo pool so fast I didn't know *what* I was seeing.' So I

OPPOSITE: *Walt was the very first Jungle Cruise skipper!* ABOVE: *Walt giving directions to Louis Francuz when the African veldt was installed on the Jungle Cruise, 1964.*

OPPOSITE: *Walt and a reporter from National Geographic hiding behind the foliage to observe guests on the Jungle Cruise, 1963.* **ABOVE LEFT:** *Walt and John Franke with one of the Audio-Animatronics "flowers that croon" in Walt Disney's Enchanted Tiki Room (pages 72 and 75).* **ABOVE RIGHT:** *Walt with the Master of Ceremonies, Jose (voiced by his good friend Wally Boag), 1963.* **BOTTOM:** *Walt playfully pretends that the tiki totem is biting his hand, 1963.*

"Walt was the first to go on the attractions. Just like a little kid. He'd get off and giggle . . ."

—MARVIN DAVIS

said, 'Walt, do you have the time to go around with me in a boat? Show me.' And he went with me through the ride and showed me what he wanted . . .

"After he left, I got with my foreman and told him, 'For the next week you and I are going to get seasick on this ride.' We spent the whole week retraining everyone. The next week, sure enough, Walt showed up. But he just walked by. So we retrained again the following week. And the next week Walt stopped at the attraction . . . but he didn't take just one ride; he rode five or six different boats. But when he stepped off the last one, he gave me a thumbs-up. He was satisfied!"

DOMINGUEZ FAMILY TREE (1895)

Landscape designer Bill Evans shares this about the second-oldest thing at Disneyland, a palm planted in 1896 by an early rancher (the grandfather of former executive vice president of Disney Attractions Ron Dominguez): "It was a stalwart and revered resident of his front lawn, admired by three generations of children and adults. One member of the family married beneath it. When the owner of the land sold his acreage [where Pirates of the Caribbean is now] to Walt Disney in 1954, he requested that this venerable palm be preserved. Walt was more than happy to oblige . . . he ordered that it be carefully 'balled,' lifted tenderly from its old home and trundled, all fifteen tons of it, to Adventureland."

The original location for the relocated palm was near the queue for the Jungle Cruise. Architectural changes around the tree—which hasn't moved—now have it standing front and center near the Indiana Jones Adventure FASTPASS entrance.

SWISS FAMILY TREEHOUSE (1962)
Re-themed as Tarzan's Treehouse (1999)

"Every kid has had dreams of living in a tree house. And the Swiss Family Robinson Treehouse probably tops those dreams . . . One of the advantages of living in a tree house is the wonderful view." —Walt

The *Disneyodendron semperflorens grandis*, or "large ever-blooming Disney tree," is the tallest at Disneyland. All three hundred thousand plastic leaves were attached by hand. And like many other attractions, it was based on one of Walt's films, *Swiss Family Robinson*.

Betty Taylor, one of the stars of the Golden Horseshoe Revue, remembers observing Walt: "One day I was having breakfast at the park just before the Swiss Family Treehouse opened for the first time. And there was Walt walking up three steps, then walking down. Then he would walk up four steps and walk back down again. He took the rope railing and shook it. He always tried things out before opening them to the public."

Shortly thereafter a reporter from *Newsweek* observed, "The ordinary-looking man with the graying mustache stood alone near a turnstile at Disneyland, watching the customers explore his latest goody—a seventy-foot-tall tree house, built on three levels, and festooned with steps and galleries. The customers liked it—the furnishings, the steps, the view from the top—and so, still alone, the world's richest uncle smiled and walked away."

"When I was a youngster, tree houses fascinated me," Walt said. "I suppose they do all youngsters. I built things in the backyard. I organized the kids of the neighborhood to build a tree house. Now I've got just the one I wanted."

WALT'S DISGUISES AND BEING RECOGNIZED IN DISNEYLAND

"You know . . . I know people who don't do another darn thing but go to the park to sit on those benches. I do it every chance I get myself—but never for long. I get spotted pretty quick and then it's autograph time."
—Walt

"When Walt toured around Disneyland, he liked to go incognito. He wanted to get in and find out what the people were saying and thinking without being Walt Disney."
—Ken Anderson

"When Mother and Father visit the park and people recognize him and crowd around him, it spoils their fun a little . . . Once he stops and begins to sign autographs, he's surrounded at once. He's even attempted a mild disguise—wearing dark glasses and a hat."
—Diane Disney Miller

"Someone told me a great story about a little girl who walked up to him near the Shooting Gallery in Frontierland and asked him if he was Walt Disney. He whispered that he was, gave her his autograph, and then chuckled and asked her not to tell anyone. That was Walt through and through."
—Wally Boag

"He spent his time going around in old clothes and meeting people and finding out how they felt about Disneyland. He would ride in the ride vehicle with them. They didn't even know it was Walt. He was so nice that they would want to know who he was, and he would say, 'I'm Walt Disney.' He astounded all sorts of people."
—Ken Anderson

"When we first arrived in California, he took me to Disneyland and it was quite amazing to have a personal tour with Walt . . . all of the visitors wanted to touch him and thank him. They felt like they knew him."
—Julie Andrews

CHAPTER EIGHT
FRONTIERLAND

"Here you can return to Frontier America. All these and many other adventures in Frontierland are designed to give you the feeling of having 'lived,' even for a short while, during our country's days of pioneer development."

—WALT

FRONTIERLAND PLAQUE AND FLAGPOLE (1955)

TO
WALT DISNEY
IN RECOGNITION OF OUTSTANDING
ASSISTANCE AND COOPERATION IN EXTENDING
HUMANE IDEALS TO PEOPLES THROUGHOUT THE WORLD
FROM
THE AMERICAN HUMANE ASSOCIATION
JULY 1955

This plaque was presented to Walt in his office in Burbank and later unveiled in Frontierland as part of the Opening Day ceremonies. Walt's love of animals extended way beyond the anthropomorphic characters he created, the True-Life Adventures animal documentaries he produced, the humane treatment of the four-legged stars in his films, and his beloved pets. (He wouldn't allow any creature to be exterminated at his home, studio, or park.) Walt's care and concern for these sentient beings were ingrained in his DNA: "It was the most natural thing in the world for me to imagine that mice and squirrels might have feelings just like mine."

"He loved the little animals," Herb Ryman adds, "the little horses, ponies, and mules—they were really the first employees at Disneyland."

Flying on the flagpole is a replica of the first official United States flag—the Stars and Stripes. Approved by Congress on June 14, 1777, it has thirteen alternating red and white stripes and thirteen stars and befits Frontierland's era. And Walt's patriotism.

Walt atop Fort Wilderness while it's under construction on Tom Sawyer Island, 1956.

"One morning before the park opened I was near the *Mark Twain* when I noticed Walt was standing outside the Golden Horseshoe. I was curious what Walt was doing, so I walked over there. Two workers were hanging a refurbished sign. Walt told them it was crooked.

"One of the workers was holding a level tool and showed it to Walt. He added, 'Sir, it is straight.'

"Walt shook his head and insisted, 'No, it's not.'

"The worker climbed the ladder and measured again. Walt was right. It wasn't straight."

—JIM CORA

THE GOLDEN HORSESHOE (1955)

This is an elaborate replica of typical saloons one would find throughout American frontier towns. The bar had the "tallest glass of pop," and Walt was clear only nonalcoholic beverages would be sold here. Prior to the attraction's debut, Walt noticed whisky bottles as set decorations on the back bar. He insisted they be removed: "We've got to change those labels on those bottles . . . there are going to be a lot of people coming in here. I would like it if they didn't see anything that anyone would disapprove of."

Walt personally hired the star of the Golden Horseshoe Revue, gag man Wally Boag. "I can't remember how many times I've seen the show," said Walt, "but I always find it stimulating to be there and watch the responses of the audience—and although I practically know the routine by heart it is always new and exciting."

Walt had a private box on the lower right side of the stage (stage left); however, he was a man of the people and was usually found on the main floor with everyone else.

Four days before Disneyland opened, Walt and Lilly hosted their thirtieth wedding anniversary at the Golden Horseshoe, following the maiden voyage of the *Mark Twain* Riverboat. As the festivities kept going, Walt was not tiring of the fun, finding his way to the upper balcony. "People below started to notice him," recalled his daughter Diane. "'There's Walt,' they said. There was a little applause and general recognition from the audience. And with that, Daddy was off. He started to climb down the balcony, and every little bit of comment or applause would just keep him onward. At one point it got a little touchy—I thought he was going to fall from the balcony. But he made it down to the stage.

"He just stood there and beamed. Everyone started saying, 'Speech! Speech!' But there was no speech forthcoming. All he did was stand there and beam. . . . He was loving every minute of it, just grinning at people."

Following the long and eventful day, Diane offered to drive her father home. "He just climbed in the back seat of the car. He had a map of Disneyland, and he rolled it up and tooted in my ear as if it were a toy trumpet. And before I knew it, all was silent. I looked around and there he was, with his arms folded around the map like a boy with a toy trumpet, sound asleep."

THE OTHER OCCUPIED APARTMENT AT DISNEYLAND

Walt wasn't the only one with an apartment at Disneyland. Golden Horseshoe star Wally Boag had one, too, located above the restaurant that is River Belle Terrace today. He

TOP: *Walt in the upper balcony box of the Golden Horseshoe before climbing down, 1955.* BOTTOM: *Sharon, Walt, Lilly, and Diane onstage with the anniversary cake, 1955.*

explains, "Walt was so good to take care of his performers, and he insisted on providing great living quarters for us. He wanted to ensure we had a comfortable place to relax between the five or six shows we did every day."

THE RIVERS OF AMERICA (1955)
"I think he took more actual interest in the river . . . than anything else."
—Marvin Davis

"When the time came to fill the Rivers of America with water, the surveyors and engineers explained to Walt that they would need a special pump to get the water from the source to the river," animator and director Wilfred Jackson recalls. "Walt said, 'No, just cut a flume here, then turn the water on.' The men said that water doesn't go uphill and this was impossible. Walt insisted. Finally, to appease their boss, they turned on the water. Sure enough, the water ran uphill to the river! What they didn't realize was that Walt had a terrific memory. He remembered the lay of the land from his orange grove visit. He knew where the source was and how the orange grower irrigated. The engineers had an error on their maps, but Walt knew better."

Disney Parks publicist Charlie Ridgway reminisces: "Walt's favorite pastime in the first years was sitting on the Rivers of America in Frontierland, looking across to Tom Sawyer Island as rafts carried guests to the adventures inspired by another famous Missourian, Mark Twain."

"Sometimes he'd sit with his sketchbook, soaking up the view," Marty Sklar adds.

Renie Bardeau, the photographer famous for taking the photo of Walt in his fire truck with Mickey Mouse riding shotgun—one of the last of Walt in Disneyland—observed him near the Rivers of America one day: "He went over to the popcorn wagon; a young lad was making popcorn . . . Walt reached in his pocket and pulled out some money and said, 'A bag of popcorn, please.'

"'Oh! Walt!'" Recognizing his boss, he offered it for free. "'Walt, here.'

"'No no no. I know that you have to account for every carton. . . . So here's the money. Gimme the popcorn.'"

After the exchange, Walt took the popcorn to the bank of the rivers. When a family of ducks swam by, he dumped the bag into the water to feed them.

MARK TWAIN RIVERBOAT (1955)
In his late teens (after serving as a Red Cross ambulance driver post World War I), Walt had planned to sail the Mississippi; while that didn't work out, his dream came true when he built his own riverboat for Disneyland. It's authentic in every detail, down to the name, which goes back to the turn of the century, before Walt's hero Samuel Clemens claimed it, when leadsmen sang their safety call, "Mark twain"—meaning the water was twelve feet deep and thus safe for the vessel to proceed.

"Come on, Roland. Let's go for a ride on the rivers." That was Walt's invitation to the young Imagineer Roland "Rolly" Crump to ride the *Mark Twain* Riverboat with his boss.

Rolly remembers vividly, "We boarded and Walt was standing there, hands on his hips. He was like a little kid, breathing in the air and looking all around.

"Everyone in the park knew each other . . . It was like a club. A private club. Just delightful. And Walt, of course, was right there leading everyone. You'd see him all over the park."

—WALLY BOAG

"If he was working, he'd be walking through the park with his old gray pin-striped pants on. He wore a beat-up leather jacket . . . and a straw hat. I saw him like that when he was building Tom Sawyer Island. When you saw him like that he was there to work. But if he was just out there meeting the guests, he'd wear his blue serge suit and his Smoke Tree tie and he'd be out there walking the park. If he was dressed like that, then he was there showing someone around or just hanging out for the sake of the guests."

—WILLIAM "SULLY" SULLIVAN

"He was taking it all in, from the banks of Frontierland to the action on Tom Sawyer Island."

Walt beamed. "You know, Rolly, if you really take a little time and let your imagination take care of you, what you're really looking at is the past!"

FOWLER'S HARBOR (1955)

"By the time Joe gets through with that damn ditch, we won't have any money left," complained Walt when he saw the unsightly excavation for the dry dock.

Joe Fowler, who retired from the U.S. Navy in 1948 only to be hired by Walt in 1954, responded, "Walt, it's just as simple as this: if we're gonna have a craft the size of the *Mark Twain* in the river, we have to have someplace to periodically overhaul the ship's bottom. There's just no question about it."

In the end, Walt was very pleased and named this location in honor of his admiral.

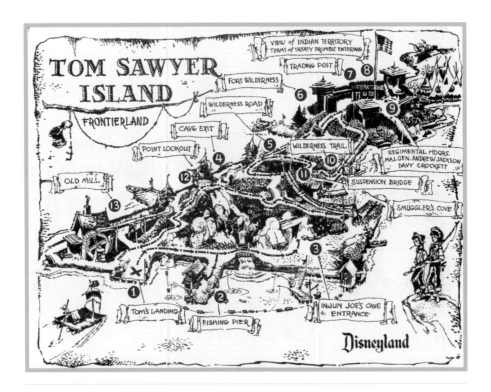

Early Tom Sawyer Island map, circa 1956.

TOP: *A quiet moment for Walt on his* Mark Twain *Riverboat in 1955. At the time, the island was there; however, the Tom Sawyer Island attraction was yet to be built.* BOTTOM: *Walt and team surveying the Rivers of America under construction, 1955.* OPPOSITE: *Walt and New Orleans mayor Victor Schiro on a Tom Sawyer raft, 1966.*

Walt and a model for the Mark Twain Riverboat, *1954. The 105-foot-long paddlewheeler was the first one built in America in fifty years. An extensive search was conducted for gimbal lights, smoke bells, and running lights authentic to the period. When funding fell short, Walt completed the project with his own funds (page 88). Admiral Joe Fowler said of Walt and his riverboat, "Yes, he loved it. There isn't any question."*

**"No steamship that ever plied the Mississippi
River was as elegant as that little jewel that
Walt built for Disneyland."**

—HERB RYMAN

TOM SAWYER ISLAND (1956)

Tom Sawyer Island has the distinction of being the only attraction Walt created all by himself. Besotted with fellow Missourian Mark Twain and his adventure novels, Walt wanted to create a playground where, as Tom Sawyer put it, "you don't need to get up early in the morning and go to school, and you never have to wash your face and hands. All you have to do is just look for treasure all day long."

Imagineer Marvin Davis recalls the evening when Walt decided to take over the design: "When I was working on the layout for . . . Tom Sawyer Island, I had done several schemes on the thing, and he came in one night and said, 'Gimme that thing.' And he took it home. He had a little drafting table in that little red barn behind his house. He came in the next morning with this legitimate piece of tracing paper and he had laid out this thing to scale, with all the little inlets and the island. He said, 'Quit fooling around and draw it the way it should be.' By God, I did. I put it down and traced it off and that's the way it is today. He literally drew it out himself."

Walt said gleefully, "I put in all the things I wanted to do as a kid—and couldn't."

"I was originally called upon to name some of the nomenclature for Tom Sawyer Island," says Herb Ryman. "Naturally, you obviously think about Smugglers Gulch and Robbers Cove and kind of inspiring names little children would be excited about. And then, later one day, as Bill Cottrell told me, he said he and Walt rode around on the *Mark Twain*. And Walt had this map in front of him where these names were allocated according to my designation. And Walt said, 'Why should we let Herbie name all these names on the island? Why can't I name these?' Bill said, 'Yes, I think you could.' So Walt renamed all these names."

Years after Walt passed away, his brother Roy recollected, "It was real simple. That was the island we played on in Marceline, Missouri. It was about twenty feet off the shore, just a little sandspit on the Mississippi. Walt and I took boxes out there and we built this fort. The fort Walt was building at Disneyland was the fort he played on as a kid. In his mind, he knew what the fort looked like and exactly where it should be. And I believe Walt thought it was real."

FISHING PIER (1956–circa mid-1960s)

Joe Fowler explains that the fishing pier was another wistful brainchild of Walt's: "When we built Nature's Wonderland, we had that river coming down, and at one time he wanted to build a farmhouse in there. He said, 'You know, this is going to be a great thing, Joe. We'll have this river going by, with all of the animation and so forth, and we'd get some live fish, too. Can you have live fish?'"

The answer, of course, was yes. The river was stocked with thirty-eight pounds of bona fide river catfish courtesy of the Mark Twain Hotel in Hannibal, Missouri. Fishing continued until the mid-sixties; its demise was in part because of the odor from guests carrying their fish around the park (before the catch-and-release policy) and efforts to keep the river's water pristine.

TOP: *Walt's sailing ship was based on a single sketch. The detail is so exact that there's a brass plaque honoring the real* Columbia's *first mate, Robert Haswell, below the center mast (page 97), 1965.* MIDDLE: *Walt and Admiral A. C. Richmond on the occasion of the belowdecks attraction opening, 1964.* BOTTOM: *Admiral Joe Fowler, Walt, Gretchen Richmond, and Alfred C. Richmond, Coast Guard commandant presenting a gift bible to the ship. June 14, 1958.*

TOP: *Testing the canoe. Pictured left to right: Joe Fowler, Dick Irvine, Bill Cottrell, Vic Greene, George Whitney, Walt Disney, Bill Evans, Ray Miller, Jack Reilly.* BOTTOM: *On the occasion of Tom Sawyer Island's dedication, contest winners Chris Winkler and Perva Lou Smith from Hannibal, Missouri (Mark Twain's birthplace) portray Tom Sawyer and Becky Thatcher, 1956.*

WALT'S DREAMING TREE IN THE LAKOTA VILLAGE

When you're a passenger on either of Walt's sailing vessels, pay special attention to the Lakota village on the riverbank. Nestled behind the large tepee and firepit is a very special tree. Botanically, it's a cottonwood, identifiable by its heart-shaped leaves. It had special meaning for Walt. Back when he was a young boy in Marceline, he used to lie under its dappled leaves and dream. He named it the Dreaming Tree, crediting it as the birthplace of his imagination.

When the Dreaming Tree was struck by lightning and destroyed, three saplings, known as Sons of the Dreaming Tree, were grown from seeds of the original. One was replanted near the original site on the Disney family farm, another in a secret location (insurance should lightning strike twice). The third was gifted to Disneyland by the Walt Disney Hometown Museum on the occasion of the park's fiftieth anniversary (and originally planted near the *Mark Twain* dock on that occasion).

SAILING SHIP *COLUMBIA* (1958)

"Typical is what happened one day when Walt and Admiral Joe Fowler, Disneyland construction supervisor, were looking over the park's Rivers of America attraction," reminisced Roy O. Disney. "It was the scene of feverish activity. The paddlewheeler *Mark Twain* was puffing around a bend. Two rafts crowded with children were crossing to Tom Sawyer's island . . . It looked as if the whole flotilla was about to converge in one huge collision.

"'Gosh, isn't that great!' Walt exclaimed. 'Do you know what we need now?'

"'Yeah,' grunted Fowler. 'A port director.'

"'No,' said Walt. 'Another *big* boat!'"

And not just any big boat. Walt chose the *Columbia* for Disneyland because, he said, "It represents one of the major achievements in American sea annals."

"During construction Walt was fascinated, and he'd come down," said Joe. "I told him, for example, that it was characteristic of the old sailing ships, before the mast was set, to put a silver dollar underneath it, as a matter of good luck. So he personally put a dollar under each one of the masts on *Columbia*."

Upon its debut, Walt proudly announced, "It was a day for celebration when the square-rigger *Columbia* was added to Disneyland's fleet. She was from an earlier era than the *Mark Twain*. The *Columbia* is a replica of the first American ship to circumnavigate the globe. The commission was signed by George Washington in 1787. She left Boston and returned nearly three years later, after having logged forty-one thousand plus miles."

The belowdecks attraction was added in 1964. Walt wanted to give guests a glimpse into how crews worked and lived while at sea during the eighteenth century.

CASA DE FRITOS (1957–1982)
Rancho del Zocalo (2001)

This building was erected for the very popular Casa de Fritos, which had outgrown its small space across the way in Frontierland (next to what is now River Belle Terrace). Adjacent was Rainbow Caverns Mine Train (later Mine Train Through Nature's Wonderland). Easily seen from the outdoor dining patio of this restaurant are relics of the Walt-era attraction, now part of Big Thunder Mountain Railroad: the dinosaur skull and most of the rib cage, along with the original town, Rainbow Ridge. The miniature buildings were a favorite of Lilly's. She and Walt enjoyed evening strolls through the Western town when they stayed overnight and the park was closed.

PIONEER MERCANTILE (1955)

Walt purchased several coin-operated orchestrions (mechanical musical machines that produce the effect of an orchestra) from collector Mrs. Raney in 1953. Mrs. Raney was quite particular and stated after the sale, "The machines found a good home, one where they will be cared for and appreciated. Otherwise I would not have sold them to Disney."

Walt installed these musical machines around Main Street to re-create the sound of the 1920s. One machine moved to Frontierland in 2015 when the Main Street train station was being refurbished. It's located in the back of the mercantile and plays for a quarter.

The only other orchestrion remaining in Disneyland is the pipe organ inside the Penny Arcade on Main Street, U.S.A.; it performs for free every seven minutes. The rest of Walt's collection was sold to collectors, save two that were sent to Walt Disney World in the early 1970s.

Walt and Lilly, 1957.

PETRIFIED TREE (1957)

This relic is the oldest thing at Disneyland—at seventy-five million years old!

Charlie Ridgway recalls the day in 1956 when Walt and Lilly were visiting the Pike Petrified Forest in Colorado: "Mrs. Disney waited impatiently in the car while Walt talked to a ranger at Petrified Forest. For her next birthday, her gift was a huge petrified stump Walt had purchased that day."

On the occasion of Walt and Lilly's thirty-second anniversary, July 13, 1957, it was installed in Frontierland.

PANCAKE HOUSE (1955–1970)
River Belle Terrace (1971)

According to Walt's daughter Diane, this was one of Walt's favorite dining spots: "When Mother and Dad would spend their weekends there, Dad had this little routine. He'd get dressed and walk the park before anyone else was there. They were still sweeping the streets and watering it down. And he had breakfast at the Pancake House. It was his neighborhood."

The Frontierland train station as it appeared in 1955. Now it sits on the opposite side of the tracks in New Orleans Square.

FRONTIERLAND TRAIN STATION (1955–1966)

This original depot was removed from service and relocated for park progress and now sits behind the tracks, on the opposite side of the passenger loading platform at the New Orleans Square station. Look closely at the ticket window and you'll see an antique telegraph sounder; it's tapping portions of Walt's Opening Day speech in Morse code.

Jim Cora shares a fun memory of when the Firehouse Five Plus Two (a band with Walt's studio personnel sidelining as musicians) performed here in the late '50s: "Ward Kimball was tiring of the conductor's announcements signaling the train's arrival while the band was playing. The next time he was asked to play, he brought wire cutters and cut the lines to the loudspeakers."

Disneyland's original Tom Sawyer, Tom Nabbe, sweetly recounts, "Walt spent a lot of time in Frontierland. I would see him there in the mornings before the park opened, sitting on the bench in front of the train station. He was kicked back with his arms stretched across the back of the bench, taking in the early morning mist and smell of lush vegetation. He seemed content sitting there in his Magic Kingdom."

The Fire House Five Plus Two, circa 1950s.

WALT'S SKETCHING AND DOODLING

"As usual, he was sketching and doodling away on little pieces of paper. Walt would take his little sketches . . . the little slips of paper he drew on . . . and he would always crumple them up and put them in his pocket. He knew that the guys sitting at the table were waiting for anything that Walt drew. He was always filling his pockets with these crumpled bits of paper so nobody in a meeting ever went away with anything."
—Bob Gurr

"When we would go out to eat, he'd take a paper napkin and tell me, 'We're going to do this and we're going to do that.'"
—Lilly Disney

"Walt would often draw on a piece of paper any kind of ideas. He would either take it over to WED and show it to the WED guys to see what they would do with it, or if he was dissatisfied with it, he would throw it away . . ."
—Ron Miller

"Walt was very interested in the overall plan of Disneyland, and two or three times he brought in a little scribble on a napkin or a piece of paper. I finally said, 'Walt, if you're going to do this, take a roll of tracing paper with you.'"
—Marvin Davis

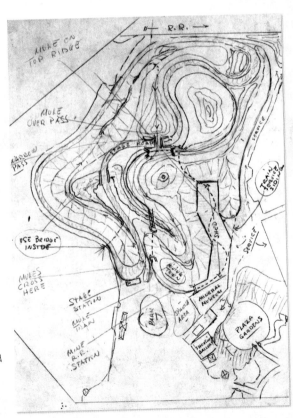

Disney Legend and Walt Disney Archives founder Dave Smith explains, "When Walt was planning this attraction, he was not satisfied with his designers' creations, so he took drawing materials home and drew up the entire ride himself. Today this drawing is one of the treasures of the Walt Disney Archives." First Rainbow Caverns Mine Train, 1956–1959, it was updated in 1960 and renamed Mine Train Through Nature's Wonderland. It closed in 1977. Big Thunder Mountain Railroad occupies the space now.

CHAPTER NINE
NEW ORLEANS SQUARE

"Disneyland has always had a big river and a Mississippi sternwheeler. It seemed appropriate to create a new attraction at the bend of the river. And so Disneyland's New Orleans Square came into being."

—WALT

Walt took several trips to New Orleans, Louisiana. He was enamored of the unique architecture of the city and asked his designers to replicate it for his brand-new land along the Rivers of America.

Herb Ryman recalls Walt's impatience with the project's progress: "Well, Herbie, I guess you guys have dropped the ball with New Orleans Square."

Herb explained that he had some ideas—and felt strongly about how it ought to be—however, it wasn't his project.

"It is now," Walt said firmly. "Do anything you wish. I'm coming back at noon tomorrow and I want my square."

Thanks to Herb, Bill Martin, and his Imagineers, Walt got exactly what he wanted: "The original architecture and atmosphere of old New Orleans of the 1850s has been retained. The narrow winding streets, intimate courtyards, and the iron-lace balconies are authentic in every detail . . ."

Walt continued, "And all these little streets are going to be very intriguing, little shops and things. And people can wander around in there. And then in here, we have a special attraction. We call it the Blue Bayou Lagoon. And people are going to get on a boat here, ride through the lagoon, and then as they get around here we are going to take 'em down a waterfall, and take 'em back into the past into the days of the pirates, you know, where the whole Caribbean area was full of pirates and they're always sacking towns and things."

This was Walt's last land. He dedicated it on July 24, 1966, and notably, it was the only land at Disneyland debuting without an attraction; Pirates of the Caribbean was still under construction. And while the adjacent Blue Bayou Restaurant was ready for business, Walt wouldn't allow it to open, because, he said, "it's a bad show to look at the bayou without the pirate boats floating by."

Walt dedicating New Orleans Square, July 24, 1966. He enjoyed visiting New Orleans, Louisana, and it is there that Audio-Animatronics characters got their start with a purchase Walt made in an antique shop. Imagineer Wathel Rogers explains, "It kind of started with Walt, and his little mechanical bird in a cage that he had. One of those that you could wind up and it would whistle . . . Walt gave it to me and asked me to look inside it."

ABOVE: *Walt with a model for New Orleans Square, 1966.* **OPPOSITE:** *Walt with the mayor of New Orleans, Victor Hugo "Vic" Schiro, 1966. Jim Cora overheard Walt playfully tell the Crescent City mayor that his New Orleans would be cleaner than his.*

TOP: *Walt shows Claude Coats the action he envisions for a scene in Pirates of the Carribean, 1965. Claude said of his boss, "Walt was not easy to work for, but he was wonderful to work with."* **BOTTOM:** *Walt reviewing a captive townsperson with Marc Davis (left) and Blaine Gibson (right), 1965.*

> **"Walt knew every nail in Disneyland. He loved to show it off to me. I remember when they were building the Pirates ride. He insisted that I walk through with him, even though it was all dirt. He put a plank down over the dust for me to walk on, because he wanted me with him."**
>
> —LILLY DISNEY

PIRATES OF THE CARIBBEAN (1967)

"This is a Caribbean town of the period, and here are the pirates and they're ransacking and carrying away loot and everything," Walt described with excitement. "Now here you see the pirates are dunking the mayor into the well, trying to force him to reveal the hiding places of the town treasure. The audience will be seeing this from a boat, you know. All the characters will be life-size. And lifelike in their movements."

Although the attraction opened a few months after Walt's passing (sadly, he never experienced the finished version), a pirate-themed attraction had been under consideration for over a decade.

Walt had tremendous influence and input on his final fully supervised attraction.

Buoyed by the success at the 1964–65 New York World's Fair and, in particular, the success of the first Audio-Animatronics human-like figure, Mr. Lincoln, Walt suggested, "So let's do a fun ride like 'the pirates.'"

But not just any fun ride. Walt was very clear to Sam McKim that the world's fair had been wonderful; however, he had set his sights much higher: "That's fine for Mach 1. But I'm thinking Mach 3."

It was first conceived as a walk-through wax museum, but concerns were raised that it would be hard to keep the guests' attention and they might skip past certain scenes; a conveyance was suggested and boats were selected.

Imagineer X Atencio remembers, "We mocked up the pirate ride auction scene in a warehouse for Walt to see. Then we rigged up a dolly with a chair and pushed him through at about the speed of the boats. As we got to the scene, the sound was playing and it was a great cacophony of pirate voices and music. I said, 'Sorry, Walt. It's hard to understand what they're saying.'

"'It's like a cocktail party,' answered Walt. 'You tune in to one conversation and then in to another. Each time guests go through, they'll hear something new and different.'"

Marc Davis adds, "Walt was around up to the point where we had programmed the animation for the auction scene. Not completely, but most of it was there. One of the last things that happened, just before Walt passed away, was the tour of our work at Disneyland. The Pirates building was up, and the water channel was walkable, all the way through. Walt, myself, and half a dozen other guys did a walk-through of the ride. There wasn't much scenery up in there, just some frameworks here and there. You could tell where you were, and Walt's reaction was very favorable. We had made the Auctioneer pirate so sophisticated that you could watch him move, and it was as good as watching Lincoln. He had all the little mouth movements and all that, and I mentioned to Walt that I thought it was a [waste]. Walt said, 'No, Marc, it's not a waste . . . we do so much return business down here, and the next time people come in they'll see something they hadn't noticed before.' That was a good example of the kind of input Walt had to these attractions."

The drop was not intended as a thrill—it was a necessity. Walt made the final decision: "We're just going to go under the railroad track and into a big building outside the berm. There are too many ideas happening that are too confined in this small space."

Walt tasked Herb Ryman: "Now this is a water ride, so it's going to go down twenty-six feet . . . can you draw some stuff to show how we're going to get down there?"

Herb did as instructed, drawing people plunging in a boat, screaming, and getting wet. When he showed the rendering to Walt, he responded, "Yeah, yeah. Mind if I take this with me?" Herb, of course, could not refuse his boss.

Walt came back the next day and said to Herb, "I changed your idea. I've got them going down. They do it once and they only go down twelve feet, and then they go along and they don't know it's going to happen again and then it happens again."

Walt concluded, "Now that's better, isn't it?"

WALT AND ROY'S APARTMENT

Walt was planning a second apartment for Roy and himself located above Pirates of the Caribbean. The gold *W* and *R* can still be seen in the wrought iron veranda above the attraction. Walt had his top designers on the job, including Emile Kuri and Dorothea Redmond. When it came to some of the furniture, though, his practical side was revealed. He explained to his pal Wally Boag about repurposing items from the set of *The Happiest Millionaire*: "I didn't make a lot of money on that picture, so I might as well get some use out of the furniture."

After Walt passed away, construction for the Disney family apartment at 21 Royal was never completed; however, it has been used for other purposes over the years, including the Disney Gallery and the Disneyland Dream Suite.

BLUE BAYOU RESTAURANT (1967)

Blue Bayou was Walt's highly anticipated themed restaurant. As early as June 1961, Walt and his Imagineers were discussing entertainment concepts for the eatery situated in eternal moonlight. Shortly thereafter Walt abandoned the idea of performers, announcing, "In this restaurant the food is going to be the show, along with the atmosphere."

Testing "up the waterfall," the conclusion of the Pirates of the Caribbean attraction, at Arrow Development in Mountain View, California.

TOP AND BOTTOM: *Riding the Pirates of the Caribbean flume mock-up are Arrow Development's Karl Bacon, Walt, and Walt's WED team, including Marc Davis, Claude Coats, Dick Nunis, Bill Martin, Dick Irvine, Don Edgren, X Atencio, Joe Fowler, and Roger Broggie, 1965.*

"All of us who worked for him recognized that he loved people," Blaine Gibson recalls, "One time a buyer came in with some chairs they were thinking of using for the Blue Bayou Restaurant, and people who came in could try them out. Walt came in and sat down on one. He looked around and said, 'We can't have these! A woman could catch her skirt on this!' Walt wanted to do what he liked, but he wanted people to be happy." Blue Bayou was the first reservation-based eatery at Disneyland; however, a table couldn't be arranged by phone. Once the park opened, guests had to go to the restaurant to secure a guaranteed dining time.

CLUB 33 (1967)

"Walt Disney's concept—an elegant
exclusive club for Very Important People . . ."

Walt was planning a private club adjacent to his new apartment to entertain dignitaries, potential sponsors for future projects, and VIPs; it was described as "a private show within a public show."

WED interior designer Tania McKnight Norris (also known for her work in the Haunted Mansion, including the iconic purple wallpaper), Bob Brown (Sharon Disney's husband), Emile Kuri, and Dorothea Redmond were responsible for the design of Club 33.

In 1965, Tania went to New Orleans with Walt—along with others, including Lilly, Roy, Edna Disney, Herb Ryman, Bill Martin, Claude Coats, and Bill Evans—to research the architecture. They also purchased the antiques and artifacts for the interior of the club. Tania recalls, "My days were spent scouring the antique shops in the Vieux Carré or Old Town, New Orleans, for antiques that would be appropriate for New Orleans Square shops and Club 33. I would take Polaroid photos for everyone to review, then Bob Brown and myself and sometimes others would go and actually purchase the items. Walt saw photos of every item, which, besides furniture, included pieces of cast iron for balconies that could be recast for use in Disneyland."

Walt had a personal space planned, too: the Trophy Room, with a masculine motif and hunting trophies provided by his friends. An Audio-Animatronics vulture was mounted on the wall. Microphones were hidden in the chandeliers, placed there with Walt's playful intention to interact with his guests.

The idea was basic magic: a cast member would be in the adjacent room, listening to the conversation and responding as the voice of the vulture.

For instance, someone might say, "I wonder what I should have for lunch." And the vulture would answer, "Have the tomato soup!" Although the show never went on in Walt's lifetime, the feathered "predator" remains perched in the club.

Walt's wishes were for an elegant experience, including cloth napkins, fine china, and classic American cuisine. Regrettably, he did not live to raise a glass here.

The original entrance, located at 33 Royal Street, was discreet, blending into the facade next to Blue Bayou with only a speaker box labeled "33" to distinguish it. (It's still there on the left side of the doorcase.) Club 33 remains in its original second-floor location; however, the entrance—now grand—has been moved to 33 Orleans Street.

One of the biggest mysteries at Disneyland is how Club 33 got its name. The 21 Club in New York City might have been an inspiration, and interestingly, when the articles of incorporation were filed with the Secretary of State of California, it was listed as "33 Club." Jim Cora, then a supervisor for Retlaw (*Walter* spelled backward and the name of the company that oversaw Walt's personal holdings, including the two attractions he

Walt serving himself coffee at Creole Café (page 112), 1965. At the time he brought espresso to Disneyland, it was quite revolutionary in America.

wholly owned—the trains and the Monorail), recalls that Retlaw employees were told thirty-three symbolized the number of sponsors and lessees at the time of New Orleans Square's dedication. While that is accurate accounting, the enigma surrounding Club 33's name prevails. Thirty-three didn't represent the number of Imagineers who created Disneyland, nor was it the number of original lessees. And even though Club 33 serves alcohol, an idea Walt initially rejected, the club wasn't assigned its address (there aren't many addresses outside Main Street, U.S.A.)—and thus the name—in order to obtain a liquor license. Walt Disney Archives founder Dave Smith said *33* refers solely to the street address on Royal Street. (The Blue Bayou's address next door is 31.)

Walt's grandson and namesake, Walter Miller, may have come upon the most sentimental theory: number 33 is in honor of Diane Disney Miller's birth year.

Regardless of 33's symbolism, the exclusive club has an extensive membership waiting list, and it is considered a coveted invitation to dine there.

CREOLE CAFÉ (1966)
Renamed Café Orleans (1972)

Walt wanted a restaurant in New Orleans Square that would serve a good strong cup of coffee. Interestingly, he chose espresso rather than the Crescent City's native chicory. He ordered the top-of-the-line, state-of-the-art Pavoni machine from Italy.

Cast members Sally Hames and Jo Ann Wheeler share, "Walt wanted to send some pictures to Mr. Pavoni in Milano, Italy, who built this espresso coffee maker. He said, 'Now let's all face the camera and say hello to Mr. Pavoni.' We were really nervous at the beginning, but Walt started talking to us and in no time we felt we had known him for a long time. It was an experience we will never forget."

The espresso machine remains on display in the café.

HAUNTED MANSION (1969)

"I'm told I'm not supposed to scare the public,
but shucks, people like to be scared."

The Haunted Mansion opened in 1969, two and a half years after Walt passed away. While he didn't live to ride in a Doom Buggy, he had influence on the attraction, the genesis of which was first discussed in 1951 while Disneyland was being planned. Walt's playful way with the macabre goes all the way back to his boyhood days in Marceline, Missouri, when he was seven or eight years old: "Roy was always my big brother and he always took care of me . . . He said, 'Walt, we've got a job washing the hearse.' So, ah, we went down to wash the hearse. Well, he did the work, and I played dead inside the hearse all day."

The Haunted Mansion exterior was built in 1962–1963, then left vacant while Walt and his Imagineers worked on the 1964 New York World's Fair. During this time, rumors circulated that Walt had moved his Disneyland residence there. Harriet Burns adds, "They just said it was a haunted mansion because they didn't want people to go there and bother Walt Disney."

From the outset Walt was very clear he wanted his Haunted Mansion to be "neat and pretty" on the outside.

"I don't want anything ghostly. I don't want anything spooky in Disneyland. Disneyland is going to be clean all the way. The hauntedness is in the interior."

Walt's directive to Marc Davis regarding the exterior was concise: "I don't want anything in Disneyland to look like we don't take care of it . . . but inside the house you can do anything you want."

Harriet Burns recalls, "We built three different-style models of the Haunted Mansion to let Walt pick from. We kept putting the scary-looking Addams Family–style model up in

Imagineer Ken Anderson, who wrote the first script for the "Haunted House," with an early model for the ballroom scene in the Haunted Mansion, 1957. "If you asked six different guys who worked for Walt," remarked Ken, "I would bet the one thing they would all say was that he was the most startling human being they ever knew."

front, but Walt always picked the style of Haunted Mansion that exists in the park today.

"Finally, we said to him, 'Walt, when we think of a haunted mansion we think of a haunted look.'

"'No, no,' he said. 'The haunting is on the *inside*. I want everything at Disneyland nice, clean, and attractive.'"

"Walt wanted it to be funny—he didn't want to scare the hell out of people!" Imagineer X Atencio noted. "He wanted to just have a good, Halloween-type show. He was very particular on the feeling of the audience he wanted; he wanted to frighten them, but he didn't want to scare them to death . . ."

Later, on his television show, Walt teased his future guests: "We haven't got the ghosts in there yet. But we are out collecting the ghosts. We're going to bring ghosts from all over the world. And we are making it very attractive to 'em, hoping, you know, they'll want to come and stay at Disneyland, so we're putting in wall-to-wall cobwebs and we guarantee 'em creaky doors and creaky floors."

The Ghost Host was played by one of Walt's favorite actors, Paul Frees; he voiced a myriad of Disney roles, including Professor Ludwig Von Drake and many of the Pirates. (And because of his rare five-octave range, he voiced the Pillsbury Doughboy, too.)

Although Walt had passed away by the time the attraction's narration was recorded, Marc Davis and X Atencio made sure that his wishes were honored. Marc would prompt during the session: "Remember Walt's old line on this thing was 'Welcome, welcome in. Well . . . come in.'"

When the Haunted Mansion opened, 999 haunts moved in, and—just as Walt wanted—they remain happy at Disneyland today.

CHAPTER TEN

FANTASYLAND

"What youngster hasn't dreamed of flying with Peter Pan over moonlit London?
Here in the 'happiest kingdom of them all' you can journey with Snow White
through the dark forest to the diamond mine of the Seven Dwarfs; flee the clutches
of Mr. Smee and Captain Hook with Peter Pan; and race with Mr. Toad in his wild
auto ride through the streets of old London Town. The time spent in this carefree
kingdom will be a dream come true—for everyone who is young at heart."

—WALT

Early on Walt admitted to confidants that Fantasyland was his favorite land. This may be because it was the embodiment of his animated film classics: "When we were planning Fantasyland, I recalled the lyrics of the song 'When You Wish Upon a Star.' The words of that melody, from our picture *Pinocchio*, inspired us to create a land where dreams 'could actually come true.'"

KING ARTHUR CARROUSEL (1955)
Walt took tremendous personal pride in the center-stage carousel, which is understandable considering the merry-go-round his daughters rode in Griffith Park was one of his inspirations for Disneyland. A merry-go-round was always at the top of his list for attractions at his magical park. Walt described the centerpiece of Fantasyland, "In the middle will be King Arthur Carrousel, with leaping horses, not just trotting, all of them leaping!" That required the standers—or stationary ones—to be retrofitted to go up and down. The carriages were removed and repurposed as cars for the Casey Jr. Circus Train.

SNOW WHITE'S ADVENTURES (1955)
Snow White's Scary Adventures (1983)
This attraction was based on Walt's groundbreaking feature-length animated film *Snow White and the Seven Dwarfs*, for which he won an Academy Special Award: one full-size

Walt with Bank of America (sponsor of "it's a small world" at Disneyland) chairman of the board, Louie B. Lundborg, 1966. Jack Lindquist asked Disney reps from all over the world to send water. "We received water from every ocean, every sea, every river. In my office. I had containers from the Danube, the Volga, the Siene—even the Amazon. The kids dumped their water into the "it's a small world" flume to signify the official opening. Mixing water from around the world, to me, epitomizes the ride," recalled Jack.

TOP: *The Motor Boat Cruise operated from 1957 to 1991. While it was very popular with children who "drove" the boats (on a track), it appears Walt was having as much fun as a kid on this trip with Joe Fowler, circa 1954.* BOTTOM: *Early in the park's development, Monstro was first imagined as a "shoot-the-chute" flume ride. That idea did not make it past concept; later it was added to Storybook Land Canal Boats. Walt with Dick Irvine in 1956.*

Oscar statuette and seven small ones. (It's worth noting that Walt still holds the record for most Oscars won by an individual.)

Walt personally named each of the Dwarfs: "I'd established a distinct personality for each of them, and to anchor those personalities down, I picked a name to fit each dwarf. For instance, I called one dwarf Dopey, because he was—well, just dopey."

Dopey never spoke simply because Walt never found the perfect voice for his youngest dwarf.

While Walt was very familiar with his screen story, he was also aware of how it might affect children seeing it in a three-dimensional setting. For many years, there was a sign outside featuring the Witch warning parents that it was scary inside. (The word *scary*—a more direct reference—was added to the attraction's name after the 1983 Fantasyland remodel.) In 2021, Snow White's Enchanted Wish debuted, featuring new magic in the fairy tale journey.

Art Director Ken Anderson, whom Walt appointed to be in charge of the dark rides in Fantasyland, recalls the moral of the Snow White story, and Walt's morals, too: "Walt has always felt that—he always had us feel that there was a magic in caring for other humans. Caring for the whole human condition. Walt was one and Roy, too, believed in good conquering evil."

Walt once put it simply: "The important thing is to teach a child that good can always triumph over evil."

PINOCCHIO'S DARING JOURNEY (1983)
While Walt was not involved in the planning of the attraction, it's based on his 1940 animated classic. The space, however, was there in 1955 as the home for the Mickey

"Walt would come around two or three times a week [to the loading dock of Casey Jr. Circus Train] and talk to me in Spanish. He spoke the language pretty well. He was a remarkable, wonderful man . . . but very humble," shares former cast member Casey Boyd.

> ## "Whenever I go on a ride, I'm always thinking of what's wrong and what can be improved."
>
> —WALT

Mouse Club Theater. Once again, Walt was ahead of his time. Beginning in 1956, the attraction featured 3D technology, which was a groundbreaking innovation in mid-century America; Walt used it to showcase his brand-new television hit, *Mickey Mouse Club*.

CASEY JR. CIRCUS TRAIN (1955)

This was initially conceived as Disneyland's first roller coaster; however, it's hard to imagine the circus train as anything other than the tame "I think I can" attraction it is today.

"That was one of the things that Walt loved better than anything," said Joe Fowler. However, mechanical issues meant it wouldn't be ready for Opening Day. Joe delivered the disappointing news: "'Walt, I'm sorry. In my humble opinion we must not open that railroad until it's safe. We'll have to design something . . .' There was a two-week delay. Walt was, of course, awfully unhappy, but instead of doing like so many men would do, lose their temper and start saying, 'Why didn't you see that ahead of time?' he said, 'Well, all right.'"

And while a ticket to ride is no longer necessary, the original ticket booth remains, disguised now as Casey's train station.

DUMBO THE FLYING ELEPHANT (1955)

Dumbo the Flying Elephant was originally developed as a takeoff on the "Pink Elephants" sequence of the film. It was decided that this segment might be a bit too scary for small children, so that concept was rethought.

The attraction debuted a month after Disneyland opened, and was dubbed the Eighth Wonder of the World, because, well, elephants could fly!

MR. TOAD'S WILD RIDE (1955)

Inspired by 1949's *The Adventures of Ichabod and Mr. Toad*, the attraction had "wild" in the name; however, Walt shied away from anything *too* wild. Mr. Toad has an interesting distinction. Walt was adamant everyone was on a first-name basis in his park, and said, "Remember I'm Walt. There's only one 'mister' in Disneyland and that's Mr. Toad." (Mr. Lincoln joined the park more than a decade later.)

PETER PAN'S FLIGHT (1955)

Walt saw his first production of *Peter Pan* as a young boy in Marceline. He went on to play the title role in school, with his brother Roy hoisting the lines so he could "fly," and he ultimately produced the animated 1953 classic.

Bob Thomas observed about this attraction, "Walt visited the tin shed [where the mock-ups of attractions were staged at the studio] every day to see how the rides were progressing. His favorite was Peter Pan, because it was an entirely new concept—a fly-through with cars suspended from the ceiling. As the rides came closer to completion, Walt himself rode them over and over again . . . If he was pleased, he got off the ride with a childlike giggle. If something went wrong, the eyebrow shot up and he muttered, 'Fix this thing and let's get this show on the road.'"

TOP: *Walt and Lilly ride the Mad Tea Party with Crown Prince Akihito and Princess Michiko of Japan, 1960.* MIDDLE: *Walt and Lilly fly on Peter Pan's Flight, 1960.* BOTTOM: *Walt examining a Mr. Toad's Wild Ride attraction vehicle with Roger E. Broggie (right).*

TOP: *Walt with Fred Joerger (left) and Wathel Rogers (middle) reviewing the Storybook Land models, November 1955.* **BOTTOM:** *Walt showing a map of his Storybook Land Canal Boats, 1955.* **OPPOSITE:** *Walt and Lilly with dignitaries King Mahendra and Queen Ratna of Nepal, 1960. Claude Coats had initially designed a ride vehicle made of playing cards for Alice in Wonderland; however, Walt said, "Do a caterpillar."*

MAD TEA PARTY (1955)
New Location (1983)
Inspired by "The Unbirthday Song" scene from *Alice in Wonderland*, Walt described this attraction, which was his cup of tea: "The Mad Tea Party is a gaily colored whirl in people-sized teacups, one of Fantasyland's happiest adventures."

ALICE IN WONDERLAND (1958)
Based on Walt's 1951 film by the same name, it was intended to be an Opening Day attraction; however, time restraints delayed it by three years. Nevertheless, Walt never lost his enthusiasm for the whimsical caterpillar adventure and described it in great detail:

"Alice in Wonderland lets the visitor share the nonsensical experiences of Lewis Carroll's bewitched heroine. Entrance is through the storied Rabbit Hole, which leads to the Upside Down Room and the Oversize Chamber, after which you'll pass into Tulgy Woods to meet the Cheshire Cat, the Mad Hatter's Tea Party, through a maze of Cards and into the fearsome presence of the Red Queen, who threatens to 'roll someone's head' with every breath."

Walt with Storybook Land Canal Boats marquee under construction, circa 1956.

Outside, the tall yellow mushroom (which the Caterpillar warned Alice would change her size) was the original ticket booth during Walt's era.

CANAL BOATS OF THE WORLD (1955)
Storybook Land Canal Boats (1956)

This attraction showcases scenes from several of Walt's animated films, and features miniatures—a passionate hobby of Walt's. Not only did he make miniatures, including his first tableau—Granny Kincaid's cabin, based on a set from his live-action movie *So Dear to My Heart*—he collected them from all over the world, proudly displaying them in his office. When time permitted, Walt assisted Imagineer Fred Joerger in the studio's model shop, making the miniatures for this attraction during the evening.

"When I was doing those stained glass windows," Harriet Burns recalled, "I had cut out three hundred sixty pieces of lead for this one great big church window, and Walt came in and picked it up—and I hadn't soldered it together! It just scattered everywhere! But that's how hands-on he was! I picked it up and said, 'Oh, no problem, Walt, no problem.' We finally learned that if Walt was coming in [to the WED Model Shop], have everything glued down because he wanted to play with it so badly! It was so marvelous to see his eyes twinkle, and to see how delighted he was with our toys—well, his toys! He did think of our place as a toy shop."

Dick Nunis commented on Walt's dedication to detail: "We were redoing the Storybook Land attraction and trying to cut its budget. One of the art directors said, 'Walt, we can just use regular glass rather than stained glass.' Walt said something profound: 'Look, the thing that's going to make Disneyland unique and different is the detail. If we lose the detail, we lose it all.'"

The lighthouse near the entrance was first a Walt-era ticket booth.

"it's a small world" (1966)
NEW YORK WORLD'S FAIR (1964–1965)

The happiest cruise that ever sailed serenaded by costumed children from around the world.

Walt had a clear vision for the attraction originally designed for UNICEF: "It's a tribute to the children of the world. And it's a little fantasy where you take a trip around the world of children in a boat. And you visit all the different countries, with all the different children of these countries with their costumes, and then a lot of toylike figures to represent other things. And these little figures dance, and sing, and finally end up with a big finale, which is like the finale in any musical, where all the children from these other lands that you've visited are all together in one, all singing in unison, and it's a big spectacular finish. It's called 'it's a small world.'"

Walt's original idea was to have the children of the world singing their own national anthems. Terrific idea in theory; however, all the different songs were stepping on each other, creating a cacophony. It became apparent the attraction needed *one* anthem.

Enter Walt's in-house songwriters, the Sherman brothers. Walt was quick and to the point: "I need something and I need it right away. It should talk about unity and understanding and brotherly love, but don't get preachy. And I need it yesterday, because it has to be translated into a whole lot of different languages." Richard Sherman adds, "We wrote the song so fast, we thought it was too simple to play for Walt . . . It seems to have turned out pretty well."

Artist and Imagineer Mary Blair, who contributed to *The Adventures of Ichabod and Mr. Toad*, *Alice in Wonderland*, *Peter Pan*, and other Disney classics, was revered by Walt for her unique use of color and styling; he asked her to assist in designing "it's a small world."

Walt and Mary Blair with an "it's a small world" model, 1966. Mary was proud to say, "Walt said that I knew about colors he had never heard of before."

(Rolly Crump ensured Mary's significant contribution to the attraction would never be forgotten: "It's neat that I was able to put a doll of Mary Blair on the Eiffel Tower. She's wearing a poncho.")

Walt chose Imagineer Alice Davis to create the costumes. When she queried Walt as to her budget per garment, his answer was precise and not at all dollar-related: "Alice! I want you to put costumes on those dolls that would make a little girl happy from the age of one to a hundred and to want that doll and dress! I have a building over there filled with bookkeepers that find the money. I want the most beautiful costumes you can make."

In 1966, the UNICEF-sponsored attraction came from the world's fair to be installed at Disneyland; however, one thing was missing: a facade. Walt was looking at the exterior, under construction, with Rolly Crump and pointed to the then empty platform (where the boats enter and exit below) and asked him what he thought should go on top. Rolly suggested bands could play on it. Walt replied, "No, Roland. Why don't you put a clock there?"

Later, when Walt looked at Rolly's model, inspired by a sketch by Mary Blair, he noticed there were only nine figures: "How many hours are there in a day? Make it twenty-four."

When the facade and clock for the attraction were complete, Walt quipped, "There are quicker and quieter ways to find out the correct time, but they are not as much fun."

MATTERHORN BOBSLEDS (1959)

Walt returned from visiting the set of *Third Man on the Mountain* in Zermatt, Switzerland. He understood that most Americans would never be able to travel to see the actual Matterhorn, so he decided to bring the Matterhorn to Disneyland.

Bob Gurr was given the assignment of designing the world's first steel, tubular roller coaster: "What Walt wanted was two tracks, intertwining with themselves, hidden inside a mountain, and, oh, by the way, a hole in the mountain because the Skyway is going to go through the Matterhorn." (When asked why there were holes in it, Walt liked to tease, "Because it's a Swiss mountain.")

"There was no criteria," continues Bob. "I just kept trying to make it work."

Joe Fowler supervised the construction of the attraction, recalling, "Walt just couldn't wait to get into the sled and come down the mountain and see how his show was affected, and he said, 'Isn't there some way, Joe, that we can come down there and you can effect some sort of braking arrangement?' I said, 'Give me a day.' And I did.

"The track itself was not joined to the stopping station; it ended in these big bunches of hay. So the first morning we started the sled halfway up to try it out the first time, and we came down and we landed in the hay. Walt said, 'Isn't there some way we can incorporate this into the final ride?' He was so excited, just like a kid.

"As soon as I had effected the pile of hay at the bottom as a matter of safety, the two of us came down, not once, but three or four times, because he was so enthusiastic. He was getting the effect he wanted from the show along the rail, but the bottom line was, he said, 'Can't we do it some way, get this pile of hay as a permanent part of the ride?' Of course, obviously, this was a little bit out of the question. But it was very effective, and as I mentioned, I think it's characteristic of Walt that rather than have somebody else take that trip down and then give a report, he himself insisted upon going down with me."

OPPOSITE TOP: *In 1935, Walt visited Strasbourg, France. Besotted with the animated figures of the astronomical clock, he drew sketches of it and attempted to climb the tower to see how it worked. Roy said of the "it's a small world" facade: "You might see that down at the park now. We have a big mechanical clock," 1965.* OPPOSITE BOTTOM: *Walt rides "it's a small world" on Opening Day with Louis B. Lundborg and guests, 1966.*

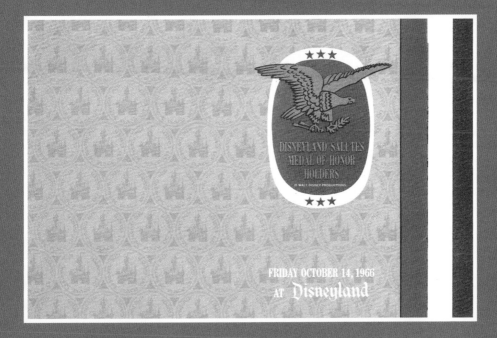

DISNEYLAND SALUTES
MEDAL OF HONOR
HOLDERS

© WALT DISNEY PRODUCTIONS

★★★

FRIDAY OCTOBER 14, 1966
AT *Disneyland*

OPPOSITE LEFT, ABOVE, AND BELOW: *The Medal of Honor is the United States' highest award for military valor in action. Established during the Civil War—with the legislation signed by Abraham Lincoln—the medal has always stood for actions that go above and beyond the call of duty.*

"Great Moments with Mr. Lincoln"

MENU OF THE DAY

Luncheon Salads

Tossed Green • Green Bean
Ambrosia • Cottage Cheese
Tomato and Avocado • Jello

Large A La Carte Salads

California Fruit • Catamaran
Chef's • Tomato filled with Tuna

Entrees

Standing Rib Roast • Fried Shrimp
Baked White Fish • English Pot Roast
Fried Chicken

All entrees include potato and two vegetables

Desserts

French Pastries • Apple Pie with Cheese
German Chocolate Cake • Banana Nut Cake
Cherry Tart

Beverages

Tea • Coffee • Milk • Pepsi-Cola
Coca-Cola • Hot Chocolate

Disneyland is privileged to have as its special guests today the holders of the Congressional Medal of Honor. We are proud to salute those Americans who have demonstrated the strength of mind and spirit that enables a man to encounter the threat of danger to himself and to his country with firmness and courage. We sincerely hope that your visit to Disneyland will be an experience you will long remember as one of personal enjoyment and satisfaction.

Walt Disney

CHAPTER FOURTEEN
HAPPILY EVER AFTER

"There is no way to replace Walt Disney. He was an extraordinary man. Perhaps there will never be another like him . . . The world will always be a better place because Walt Disney was its master showman."

—ROY O. DISNEY

"I was working down by the Matterhorn and he was going around all by himself," said Disneyland cast member Joyce Ballenger. "He'd stop, and he'd look at each of the rides. He'd look it over and look it over from the outside. Then he'd turn, and he'd look at another one and so on and so forth . . . [soon thereafter] he went into the hospital. And so I felt that he was just saying good-bye, that he really loved the park."

Walt's good friend and Golden Horseshoe performer Wally Boag describes the sentiment at Disneyland the day Walt died: "There was some discussion as to whether or not the park should be closed that day, but management decided, and rightly so, that Walt would not have wanted his park closed—he always said that the show must go on. And so it did—but we were so sadly diminished without his leadership, genius, and whimsy. It was a sad event when the Disneyland band marched down Main Street that afternoon to lower the flag and slowly played 'When You Wish Upon a Star.'"

"Dick Nunis called everybody into the office and let us know that Walt had passed away, with big tears streaming down his face. We all were concerned what was going to happen," recalls William "Sully" Sullivan. "There was a discussion about what we should do and whether we should close the park that day, but the answer was no, because we knew that's not what Walt would have wanted. He wouldn't want to close the park with all the guests who had made a special trip to be there."

In 1963, *National Geographic* asked Walt, "What happens when there is no more Walt Disney?"

Walt answered, "I think about that. Every day I'm throwing more responsibility to other men. Every day I'm trying to organize them more strongly.

"But I'll probably outlive them all," he said with a grin. "I'm sixty-one. I've got everything I started out with except my tonsils, and that's above average. I plan to be around for a while."

Walt in his Nash Rambler "Cross Country" station wagon, circa 1954.

In an interview with KNBC's Bob Wright on August 24, 1966, Walt replied to the same query about his succession: "Well, I think by this time my staff, my young group of executives, and everyone else are convinced Walt is right. That quality will win out. And so I think they're going to stay with that policy because it's proved that it's a good business policy. Give the people everything you can give them. Keep the place as clean as you can keep it. Keep it friendly, you know. Make it a real fun place to be. I think they're convinced and I think they'll hang on . . . if . . . as you say . . . well . . . after Disney."

Walter Elias Disney
December 5, 1901–December 15, 1966

NOT THE END

"Whenever I see Mickey Mouse I have to cry. Because he reminds me so much of Walt."

—LILLY DISNEY

"I want them to remember him as he was. Remember the man he was. A lot of people don't know that there was a Walt Disney. They think it's a company logo and that's it. He was a good man and I want people to know that."

—DIANE DISNEY MILLER

"I never dreamed that Walt Disney would die. I didn't think they would let him."

—WALT'S SECRETARY LUCILLE MARTIN

"Walt left the world a thousand times better than when he arrived. He personified Schweitzer's quote: 'Do something good. Someone may imitate it.'"

—RAY BRADBURY

"It would not surprise me one bit if the hovering spirit of Walter Elias Disney, eyebrow raised, fingers tapping, is busy monitoring progress at all the Disney parks."

—JAMES W. ROUSE

"They [radio hosts] announced Walt's passing and then they cut in Julie Lennon's voice and she sang the Mickey Mouse Club Song: M-I-C- K-E-Y- M-O-U-S-E. I had to pull off the road. Because my tears were blinding my ability to drive."

—BUDDY EBSEN

"He was an original. Not just an American original, but an original, period. He was a happy accident, one of the happiest this century has experienced . . . He probably did more to heal or at least to soothe troubled human spirits than all the psychiatrists in the world. There can't be many adults in the allegedly civilized parts of the globe who did not inhabit Disney's mind and imagination at least for a few hours and feel better for the visitation . . . But what Walt Disney seemed to know was that while there is very little grown-up in every child, there is a lot of child in every grown-up. To a child, this weary world is brand-new, gift wrapped. Disney tried to keep it that way for adults . . . People are saying we will never see his like again."

—ERIC SEVAREID

WHY DISNEYLAND WILL NEVER WORK

"Walt's screwy ideas about cleanliness and great landscape maintenance are economic suicide. He will lose his shirt by overspending on things the customers never really notice."

"Custom rides will never work. They will cost too much to buy and they will be constantly breaking down, resulting in reduced ride capacity and angry customers. Only stock off-the-shelf rides are cheap enough and reliable enough to do the job. And besides, the public doesn't know the difference or care."

"Most of Mr. Disney's proposed park produces no revenue, but it will be expensive to build and maintain. Things like the Castle and Pirate Ship are cute, but they aren't rides so there is no economic reason to build them."

"Town Square is loaded with things that don't produce revenue, like the Town Hall, the Fire Department, and the Square itself."

"There is too much wasteful landscaping."

"The interior finishing concepts of the restaurants are too expensive, especially since a hot dog and a beer are all anyone eats at an amusement park."

"You'll lose money providing all those little design details and nice finishes. People will vandalize the ride vehicles and destroy the grounds no matter what you do, so you may as well go cheap."

"Walt's design only has one entrance. This will create a terrible bottleneck."

"Bottom line, Mr. Disney's park idea is too expensive to build and too expensive to operate. Tell your boss to save his money. Tell him to stick to what he knows and leave the amusement business to people who know it.'"

ABOVE: In his biography, Buzz Price recounts opinions from leading amusement park operators regarding the then unbuilt Disneyland. LEFT: Walt with an early map painting of Disneyland created by Peter Ellenshaw.

DREAM DOERS

"To develop Disneyland from a long-cherished dream to a reality took the skills and talents of hundreds of artists, craftsmen, architects, engineers, and scientists, to all of whom I am sincerely indebted. . . . I want to pay tribute to the many . . . whose untiring efforts helped bring this dream into a reality. Without their skills and imagination, Disneyland would not have been possible."

—WALT

Walt said it best. And I'd like to add that there are many, many more studio artists, craftspeople, engineers—and Imagineers and cast members—who aren't a part of this book. Thank you all for your contributions to Disneyland. While you may not appear on these pages, your legacy lives on in Walt's original Magic Kingdom.

Talent Biographies Presented by
D23: The Official Disney Fan Club

ANDERSON, KEN (1909–1993)
Artist; began his Disney career in 1934, contributing to many animated classics as art director beginning with *Snow White and the Seven Dwarfs*. With his architectural background, he came up with innovative perspectives on such Silly Symphony cartoons as *The Goddess of Spring* and *Three Orphan Kittens*. He specialized in character design in later years and his work included Shere Khan in *The Jungle Book* and Elliott in *Pete's Dragon*. He was production designer on such films as *Sleeping Beauty*, *One Hundred and One Dalmatians*, and *The Aristocats*. He also designed many parts of Disneyland, including major portions of Fantasyland, the Storybook Land Canal Boats, and others. He retired in 1978, but continued to consult at WED Enterprises. Anderson was honored with the Disney Legends award in 1991.

ARROW DEVELOPMENT:
ED MORGAN AND KARL BACON
Ed Morgan and Karl Bacon were two of the founders of Arrow Development, located in Mountain View, California. Walt approached Arrow Development in 1953 and commissioned them to build six attractions, which debuted on Disneyland's opening day in 1955. The attractions were Mad Tea Party, Snow White's Adventures, Mr. Toad's Wild Ride, King Arthur Carrousel, Dumbo the Flying Elephant, and the Casey Jr. Circus Train. In the following years, they continued to work with WED Enterprises (now Walt Disney Imagineering) and assisted in the development of Pirates of the Caribbean and tubular steel track breakthroughs many roller coasters feature today (not just at the Disney parks, but other parks as well).

ATENCIO, FRANCIS X. (1919–2017)
He joined Disney in 1938 as an in-betweener and became an assistant animator on *Fantasia*. X (the *X* stands for Xavier; he was called X ever since high school pals gave him that nickname) worked on the inventive *Noah's Ark*, *Jack and Old Mac*, and *A Symposium on Popular Songs*, using stop-motion animation in collaboration with Bill

Justice. In 1965, he moved to WED Enterprises, where he worked on Primeval World, Pirates of the Caribbean, Adventure Thru Inner Space, and the Haunted Mansion. For the Disneyland attractions, Atencio wrote the words for "Yo Ho (A Pirate's Life for Me)" and "Grim Grinning Ghosts." He retired in 1984, and was named a Disney Legend in 1996.

BARDEAU, RENIE (1934–2021)
Upon joining the company in 1959 as a part-time employee, one of Renie Bardeau's first assignments was to photograph Walt opening Tomorrowland with then U.S. vice president Richard Nixon. One of his most iconic photos is of Walt in a fire truck with Mickey in front of Sleeping Beauty Castle. He later became chief photographer at Disneyland (in 1968) after having captured many photos of Walt with his celebrity friends at the park.

BLAIR, MARY (1911–1978)
Started at Disney in 1940 as a story artist and went on the 1941 Disney trip to Latin America with her husband, Lee. Many of her color concepts are obvious in *Saludos Amigos* and *The Three Caballeros*. She later moved over to WED Enterprises, where she was instrumental in the design of "it's a small world." She designed two large tile murals for Tomorrowland in Disneyland and another for the Contemporary Resort at Walt Disney World. She was named a Disney Legend posthumously in 1991.

BOAG, WALLY (1920–2011)
Longtime comedian from the Golden Horseshoe Revue at Disneyland, which put him into the Guinness *Book of World Records* for the most number of performances of a show. He was most known for creating characters out of balloons and for spitting out a seemingly inexhaustible number of his "teeth" (beans) after being hit in the mouth. He opened the show at Disneyland in 1955, then took time out to get the same show started at the Diamond Horseshoe in Magic Kingdom Park at Walt Disney World in 1971 before returning to Disneyland for the remainder of his career. His last performance before his retirement was on January 28, 1982. Boag also had brief roles in *The Absent-Minded Professor*, *Son of Flubber*, and *The Love Bug*. He was named a Disney Legend in 1995.

BROGGIE, ROGER E. (1908–1991)
Broggie began his Disney career in 1939 in the Camera Department and later established the Disney Studios machine shop. Being interested in trains, he helped Walt Disney with his train hobby and engineered the layout for the scale-model train in Disney's Holmby Hills backyard. Broggie later headed MAPO and retired in 1975. One of the locomotives on the Walt Disney World Railroad is named after him. He was named a Disney Legend in 1990.

BROWN, ROBERT B. (1928–1967)
Robert was the first husband of Walt's youngest daughter, Sharon. They were married in 1959 and shared a daughter, Victoria. An interior designer by trade, Robert was part of the New Orleans Square design team.

BURNS, HARRIET (1928–2008)
She joined the Disney Studios as a set and prop painter in 1955 and later was the first woman employed by WED Enterprises, where she helped design and build prototypes for theme park attractions, and then create elements of the attractions themselves. She retired in 1986, and was named a Disney Legend in 2000.

COATS, CLAUDE (1913–1992)
Hired by Disney in 1935 as a background painter, he worked on such films as *Snow White and the Seven Dwarfs, Fantasia, Dumbo, Saludos Amigos, Make Mine Music, Lady and the Tramp, Cinderella,* and *Peter Pan.* In 1955, he moved over to WED Enterprises where he helped design Pirates of the Caribbean, the Haunted Mansion, the Submarine Voyage, the Grand Canyon and Primeval World dioramas, and for Walt Disney World the Mickey Mouse Revue, Universe of Energy, Horizons, World of Motion, and several World Showcase pavilions. He was one of the first few Disney cast members to receive a 50-year service award. He retired in 1989, and received the Disney Legends Award in 1991.

CONLEY, RENIÉ (1901–1992)
Renié was brought on by Walt to assist in designing the original Disneyland cast member costumes. She had worked as a costumer for films such as *The Big Fisherman* (1959) and and 20th Century Fox's *Cleopatra* (1963), for which she won an Oscar in 1964. Conley's lasting Disney legacy can still be found at the park with a window above the Carnation Café on Main Street, U.S.A. bearing her name.

CORA, JIM (1937–2021)
He joined Disneyland as an attraction host in 1957 and after college moved into positions of increasing responsibility in management at the park. In 1971 he assisted in the opening of Walt Disney World, and in 1979 he became involved with operations planning for Tokyo Disneyland. He later headed Disneyland International, the division responsible for liaisons between American and Disney parks abroad. He retired in 2001 after forty-three years with Disney. He was named a Disney Legend in 2005.

COTTRELL, BILL (1906–1995)
President of Retlaw Enterprises, the Walt Disney family corporation from 1964 until his retirement in 1982. He joined Disney in 1929 as a cameraman, then worked as a cutter and animation director before moving into the Story Department. He was a sequence director on *Snow White and the Seven Dwarfs* and worked on story on *Pinocchio, Saludos Amigos, Victory Through Air Power, The Three Caballeros, Melody Time, Alice in Wonderland,* and *Peter Pan.* Bill also went on the 1941 Disney trip to South America.

In 1952, he became vice president and later president of WED Enterprises, where he helped to develop the *Zorro* television series and assisted Walt Disney in the planning and construction of Disneyland. He was the first person to receive a fifty-year Disney service award, and was named a Disney Legend in 1994.

CRUMP, ROLLY
Imagineer, joined Disney in 1952 originally as an inbetweener and assistant animator. He later moved into show design at WED Enterprises, and was a key designer on the Disney attractions for the 1964–1965 New York World's Fair. He left the company in 1970 but returned several times, as a project designer for EPCOT and an executive designer for Innoventions, among other projects. He retired in 1996. In 2004, he was named a Disney Legend.

DAVIS, ALICE
She joined Disney in 1959, designing a costume for the live-action model for *Sleeping Beauty,* and went on to design costumes for *Toby Tyler.* Her primary work was the researching, designing, and dressing of the animated figures in the "it's a small world" and Pirates of the Caribbean attractions. She was the wife of Disney Legend Marc Davis (married in 1956). Alice was named a Disney Legend in 2004.

DAVIS, MARC (1913–2000)
Animator/designer; known as one of Disney's "Nine Old Men," Davis began his career at the studio in December 1935, working on *Snow White and the Seven Dwarfs.* He developed such memorable characters as young Bambi and Thumper, and gained a reputation for animating such distinctive female characters as Cinderella, Tinker Bell, and Cruella De Vil, among others. In addition, he played an active role in the planning of Disneyland and all four of Disney's 1964–1965 New York World's Fair attractions. Davis developed story and character concepts for many Disneyland attractions, including Pirates of the Caribbean, the Haunted Mansion, and "it's a small world" and later consulted on attractions for EPCOT and Tokyo Disneyland after his retirement in 1978. He was honored with the Disney Legend award in 1989.

DAVIS, MARVIN (1910–1998)
Designer; joined WED Enterprises in 1953 to help in the conceptualization and architectural design of Disneyland. He was later an art director on such films and TV presentations as *Zorro, The Swamp Fox, Moon Pilot, Babes in Toyland,* and *Big Red* and in 1964 won an Emmy for the art direction and scenic design for *Walt Disney's Wonderful World of Color.* In 1965, he returned to WED to work as a project designer on the concept for Walt Disney World. In addition to the master plan for the resort, he concentrated on the design of the hotels. He retired in 1975, and was named a Disney Legend in 1994.

DISNEY, ROY OLIVER
Walt Disney's older brother, who founded the Disney company in partnership with Walt in 1923. Born June 24, 1893; died December 20, 1971. Served as president of Walt Disney Productions from 1945 to 1968 and chairman of the board from 1964 until 1971. Roy was recuperating in Los Angeles from tuberculosis in 1923 when Walt persuaded him to join in the new venture of making animated cartoons. Roy was the financial genius of the two brothers; Walt was the creative one—and the two of them made a great pair. Modest and unassuming, Roy generally stayed in the background, finding the money for Walt's projects. It was Roy who managed the growth of

licensing Disney consumer products. He was instrumental in deciding to break with outside distributors and form the Buena Vista Distribution Company in 1953. But it was only after Walt's death in 1966 that Roy took a major public leadership position in the company and supervised the building of Walt Disney World. Through his financial acumen, that $400 million project opened in 1971, with the company having no outstanding debt. Roy was at Walt Disney World for the grand opening in October, and died two months later. In 1976, a new office building at the Disney Studios in Burbank was named the Roy O. Disney Building in honor of the company's co-founder.

ELLENSHAW, PETER (1913–2007)

Selected by Walt Disney in England to paint the mattes for *Treasure Island* and the other Disney films made there in the early 1950s. He later came to the States to work on *20,000 Leagues Under the Sea*, *Darby O'Gill and the Little People*, and other films. He painted one of the original layouts for Disneyland on a 4×8-foot storyboard, which is on display in the Disney Gallery at Tokyo Disneyland. He received an Oscar for Special Visual Effects in *Mary Poppins*. Later he served as production designer on *Island at the Top of the World* and *The Black Hole*. He was named a Disney Legend in 1993.

EVANS, MORGAN ("BILL") (1910–2002)

With his brother, Jack, he designed the landscaping for Walt Disney's home in the early 1950s, and Walt then selected him to continue the same work for Disneyland. He became director of landscape design for WED Enterprises and worked on all of the Disney parks, even consulting after his retirement. He was named a Disney Legend in 1992.

FERRANTE, ORLANDO

Imagineer who joined the Disney staff in 1962. Beginning with the Enchanted Tiki Room, he was involved with the installation of many Disneyland and Walt Disney World attractions. In 1966 he set up a department named PICO (Project Installation and Coordinating Office), and six years later moved into Imagineering administration. Ferrante retired in 2002 after helping with engineering, production, and installation at Disneyland Paris, Disney Cruise Line, and Tokyo DisneySea. He was named a Disney Legend in 2003.

FOWLER, JOSEPH ("JOE") (1894–1993)

Retired Navy admiral, chosen in 1954 by Walt Disney to oversee the building of Disneyland. He remained to be in charge of construction of Walt Disney World. He retired in 1972, and received the Disney Legends Award in 1990.

GIBSON, BLAINE (1918–2015)

Artist and sculptor, joined Disney in 1939 as an inbetweener and assistant animator, working on the features through *One Hundred and One Dalmatians*. In 1954 he began working on projects at WED Enterprises in his spare time, and went over there permanently in 1961. He headed the sculpture department, responsible for many of the heads of the Audio-Animatronics characters, from pirates to U.S. presidents. His statue of Walt and Mickey graces the hub at Disneyland. He retired in 1983, and was made a Disney Legend in 1993.

GOFF, HARPER (1912–1993)

Artist and production designer; at Disney he was also the story man for *20,000 Leagues Under the Sea*, for which he designed the *Nautilus*. He later worked at WED Enterprises on the designs for Main Street, U.S.A. and the Jungle Cruise at Disneyland, and created the layout

for World Showcase at Epcot. He was a member of the Firehouse Five Plus Two, playing the banjo. He died in 1993, the same year he was named a Disney Legend.

GRACEY, YALE (1910–1983)

Special effects expert; joined Disney in 1939 as a layout artist on *Pinocchio* and *Fantasia*. He moved to WED Enterprises in 1961, where he created special effects and lighting for the Haunted Mansion and Pirates of the Caribbean, among other attractions. He retired in 1975, and was named a Disney Legend posthumously in 1999.

GREEN, VIC

An art director with WED, he contributed designs to a number of Disneyland attractions including Great Moments with Mr. Lincoln and the Haunted Mansion.

GURR, BOB

Imagineer who specialized in vehicle design, first being retained by Disney in 1954 to consult on the design of the Autopia cars. At WED Enterprises, he worked on designs for such attractions as the Monorail, Matterhorn Bobsleds, Flying Saucers, and the antique cars and double-decker buses utilized on Main Street, U.S.A. He retired in 1981. He was named a Disney Legend in 2004.

HENCH, JOHN (1908–2004)

Artist/designer; started in the Disney Story Department in 1939, later painting backgrounds for the "Nutcracker Suite" segment of *Fantasia*. He worked on *Cinderella* and *Alice in Wonderland*, and aided Salvador Dalí in the aborted *Destino* project. Hench also worked on the special effects in *20,000 Leagues Under the Sea*. In 1955, he moved to WED Enterprises to work on the Tomorrowland area at Disneyland. He was named executive vice president of WED in 1972. Hench is known for painting the company's official portraits of Mickey Mouse for his twenty-fifth, fiftieth, sixtieth, seventieth, and seventy-fifth birthdays. In 1999, at the age of ninety, he passed his sixtieth year with the company, which was longer than any other person up to that point. He was named a Disney Legend in 1990.

IRVINE, DICK (1910–1976)

He worked as an art director at Disney in the 1940s, then returned in 1953 to head the team of designers, artists, architects, and engineers in planning and developing Disneyland. He headed WED Enterprises and continued to be in charge of planning and design for all park and World's Fair projects until his retirement in 1973. He received a Disney Legends award in 1990.

JACKSON, WILFRED ("JAXON") (1906–1988)

He joined Disney in 1928 and worked on *Steamboat Willie*. He served as an animator, director, and as producer-director on the *Disneyland* television show. Jackson pioneered a method of pre-timing animation with sound, and invented the bar sheet to coordinate the animation action with the soundtrack. Several of the cartoons he directed were honored with Academy Awards. He also worked as a sequence director on eleven features from *Snow White and the Seven Dwarfs* to *Lady and the Tramp*. Jackson retired in 1961, and was honored posthumously as a Disney Legend in 1998.

JOERGER, FRED (1913–2005)

As an Imagineer from 1953 until his retirement in 1979, Fred crafted three-dimensional models for park attractions, as well as for motion pictures. He had a special knack for creating decorative rockwork out of plaster. After his retirement, he returned to Disney as field art director for the building of EPCOT. He was named a Disney Legend in 2001.

KIMBALL, WARD (1914–2002)

Animator; began his Disney career in 1934, known as one of Walt's "Nine Old Men." He animated on such Disney classics as *Pinocchio* (on which he was noted for his creation of Jiminy Cricket), *Dumbo*, *The Three Caballeros*, and directed the Academy Award-winning shorts, *Toot, Whistle, Plunk and Boom*, and *It's Tough to Be a Bird*. He also produced episodes for the television series *Disneyland*, most notably the shows on the subject of Man in Space, and consulted on World of Motion for Epcot. Ward was a train enthusiast, whose love of the hobby helped get Walt himself interested. He was honored with the Disney Legends award in 1989.

KURI, EMILE (1907–2000)

He joined Disney in 1952 as head decorator. Kuri worked on *20,000 Leagues Under the Sea*, winning an Oscar. He supervised the set decoration on such films as *The Absent-Minded Professor*, *Mary Poppins*, *Bedknobs and Broomsticks*, and *Million Dollar Duck*, and helped decorate company executive offices and interior and exterior settings at Disneyland and Walt Disney World.

LINDQUIST, JACK (1927–2016)

Lindquist began at Disneyland in 1955 as its first advertising manager. He later took other marketing positions, and was named marketing director of both Disneyland and Walt Disney World in 1971. He brought the Pigskin Classic to Anaheim. In October 1990, he was named president of Disneyland. He retired in 1993 and was named a Disney Legend in 1994.

MARTIN, BILL (1917–2010)

Designer; joined Disney in 1953 to aid in the design effort for Disneyland. He was associated with such attractions as Snow White's Scary Adventures, Peter Pan's Flight, Nature's Wonderland, the Monorail, the Submarine Voyage, Pirates of the Caribbean, and the Haunted Mansion. He was named vice president of design at WED Enterprises in 1971, and assumed responsibility for the master layout of Magic Kingdom Park at Walt Disney World. He helped design Cinderella Castle, the riverboats, and the Utilidors beneath the Magic Kingdom. Bill retired in 1977, but returned to WED (later WDI) as a consultant on EPCOT and Tokyo Disneyland. He was named a Disney Legend in 1994.

MATHESON, BOB (1934–2020)

Beginning at Disneyland as a sound coordinator in 1960, he was later selected by Walt Disney to manage Disney's four shows at the New York World's Fair. Involved in the early planning of Walt Disney World, he moved to Florida in 1970 as director of Operations. He became vice president of Operations in 1972, vice president of Magic Kingdom/Epcot in 1984, and executive vice president of Walt Disney World in 1987. He retired in 1994, and was named a Disney Legend in 1996.

MCKIM, SAM (1924–2004)

McKim started at Disney in 1955 as a conceptual artist for Disneyland. He sketched attractions for Main Street, U.S.A. and Frontierland as well as worked on Disney films such as *Nikki, Wild Dog of the North* and *The Gnome-Mobile*. McKim contributed sketches for such Disneyland favorites as Great Moments with Mr. Lincoln, "it's a small world," the Haunted Mansion, the Monorail, and the Carousel of Progress. For Walt Disney World, he worked on The Hall of Presidents, Universe of Energy, and the Disney-MGM Studios Theme Park (known today as Disney's Hollywood Studios). He retired in 1987. McKim had been charged

with creating many of the Disneyland maps that were sold to guests through the years, and they were so highly regarded that he was persuaded to come out of retirement to design a map for Disneyland Paris. He was named a Disney Legend in 1996.

NABBE, TOM

As Disneyland's youngest cast member, he began work there in July 1955 as a "newsie" on Main Street, U.S.A. before being selected by Walt Disney to portray Tom Sawyer on Tom Sawyer Island in 1956. Later Nabbe worked on other attractions, transferring to Walt Disney World in 1971. He retired in 2003 as manager of distribution services for the Florida resort. Nabbe was named a Disney Legend in 2005.

NORRIS, TANIA MCKNIGHT

Tania joined WED in 1964. She was an interior designer for all projects apart from film. Her first assignment was New Orleans Square. Tania traveled with Walt and Roy O. (and their families) to New Orleans to do research and purchase antiques for the new area, as well as for Club 33. Tania's last major project was decorating the Haunted Mansion in Disneyland; she also designed the now famous purple wallpaper. In addition, Tania worked on parts of exhibitions for Montreal's Expo 67, concepts for Walt Disney World, and the Disney company airplane.

NUNIS, DICK

He began his Disney career in the summer of 1955 at Disneyland as an assistant to Van France in orientation training. He worked up through the ranks as area supervisor, supervisor of the mail room and steno pool, director of Disneyland operations (1961), and vice president of Disneyland operations (1968). In 1972 he became executive vice president of both Disneyland and Walt Disney World, and president in 1980. He was a member of the Disney board of directors from 1981 to 1999, and was named chairman of Walt Disney Attractions in 1991. He retired in 1999, and was named a Disney Legend the same year.

PENFIELD, ROBERT DAVE

Bob is an original "Disneylander," a term for those who began working at Disneyland on Opening Day. Employee #241, Bob stayed for forty-two years. He held many positions, including ride operator and ride foreman. He kept moving up the company ladder, taking on roles ranging from operations supervisor to field superintendent of Project Management.

PRICE, HARRISON ("BUZZ") (1921–2010)

A research economist, he was given the task, while working for Stanford Research Institute, of determining the economic feasibility and surveying the ideal location for Walt Disney's Disneyland park. In 1958, Walt Disney encouraged him to form his own company, which became Economics Research Associates (ERA). ERA was involved in many studies leading to the building and expansion of Walt Disney World, and others for CalArts, Mineral King, and Tokyo Disneyland. He was named a Disney Legend in 2003.

REDMOND, DOROTHEA (1910–2009)

A painter and illustrator at WED Enterprises beginning in 1964, Dorothea is best known for her interior settings for New Orleans Square. She later worked on Walt Disney World; one of her designs was for the elaborate murals in the entry passage through Cinderella Castle. She retired in 1974 and was named a Disney Legend in 2008.

RIDGWAY, CHARLIE (1923–2016)
Publicity director for Walt Disney World beginning two years before its opening. He had earlier started in publicity at Disneyland in 1963. Ridgway was instrumental in arranging for so much free publicity for the opening of Walt Disney World that paid advertising was felt unnecessary. He oversaw all of the major press events for the openings of Walt Disney World parks and hotels over the next two decades, retiring in 1994. He was named a Disney Legend in 1999.

RIGDON, CICELY (1923–2013)
After joining Disneyland as a ticket seller in 1957, she joined the tour guide department in 1959, being responsible for initiating its growth and development, and later all of Guest Relations and ticket sales. From 1982 until her retirement in 1994, she headed the Disneyland Ambassador program. She was named a Disney Legend in 2005.

ROGERS, WATHEL (1919–2000)
Artist/sculptor; started at Disney in 1939 in animation, and sculpted on his own time. He animated on feature films between *Pinocchio* and *Sleeping Beauty*, and created props and miniatures for such films as *Darby O'Gill and the Little People* and *The Absent-Minded Professor* and television shows such as the *Mickey Mouse Club* and *Zorro*. In 1954, Wathel was one of three founding members of the WED model shop, where he assisted in the construction of architectural models for Disneyland. He participated in Project Little Man, leading to Audio-Animatronics figures, which he programmed for many years for Disneyland, Walt Disney World, the New York World's Fair, and EPCOT attractions. Rogers retired in 1987. He was named a Disney Legend in 1995.

RYMAN, HERB (1910–1989)
Art director and designer; Herbert Dickens Ryman came to the studio in 1954 to help Walt Disney by drawing the original concept for Disneyland so Roy O. Disney could use it to help attract investors. He designed Sleeping Beauty Castle for Disneyland and over the years worked on various Imagineering projects until he retired in 1971, but he continued on after that as a consultant. He was working on Euro Disneyland plans when he died in 1989. Lithographs of a number of his concept paintings have been sold by the Disney Gallery at Disneyland. He was named a Disney Legend posthumously in 1990.

SHELLHORN, RUTH PATRICIA (1909–2006)
Ruth was a Los Angeles-based landscape architect known for the development of the "Southern California Look." She was part of the landscaping team brought in to work on Disneyland in 1955, designing the formal Victorian plan for Main Street, the Town Square, and the Plaza, among other elements.

SHERMAN, RICHARD M., AND ROBERT B. (ROBERT—1925–2012)
Songwriters; known primarily for their Disney work, they first wrote pop songs for Annette Funicello, beginning with "Tall Paul." The record sold seven hundred thousand singles. Later they wrote songs for Disney films such as *The Parent Trap*, *Summer Magic*, *Winnie the Pooh and the Honey Tree*, *That Darn Cat!*, *The Jungle Book*, *The Aristocats*, *Mary Poppins*, *The Happiest Millionaire*, *Bedknobs and Broomsticks*, and *The Tigger Movie*. It was their songs for *Mary Poppins* that gave them their big break, and two Academy Awards. In all, they wrote over two hundred songs featured in twenty-seven films and two dozen television productions, and received nine Academy Award nominations. Some of their most popular songs include "Supercalifragilisticexpialidocious," "A Spoonful of Sugar," "I Wan'na Be Like You," and "Winnie the Pooh." Probably their best-known song was not for a film at all, but for a Disney attraction at the 1964–1965 New York World's Fair—"It's a Small World (After All)." Also for the fair, they wrote "There's a Great Big Beautiful Tomorrow" for the GE Carousel of Progress. Some of their last Disney projects were songs for EPCOT in 1982. They were named Disney Legends in 1990. In 1992 Disney Records released a special retrospective collection on CD entitled *The Sherman Brothers: Walt Disney's 'Supercalifragilistic Songwriting Team*. A documentary, *The Boys: The Sherman Brothers' Story*, was released in 2009. They were portrayed in *Saving Mr. Banks*. Robert passed away in 2012.

SKLAR, MARTY (1934–2017)
Vice chairman of Walt Disney Imagineering, involved with concepts and writing contributions for most Disney theme park shows. He joined Disney in 1956, and helped develop *Vacationland* magazine. He moved over to WED Enterprises in 1961 to develop shows for the New York World's Fair. Sklar became a vice president, concepts/planning of WED in 1974, was made vice president of creative development in 1979, and in 1982 became executive vice president. He was named president in 1987. He was promoted to vice chairman when Walt Disney Imagineering and Disney Development Company merged in 1996. He had originally worked at Disneyland for a month in 1955 while a UCLA student. He was named a Disney Legend in 2001. Sklar retired on July 17, 2009, the same day a window was dedicated to him on City Hall in Town Square at Disneyland.

SULLIVAN, WILLIAM ("SULLY")
He joined the staff at Disneyland in 1955, progressing from ticket taker to ride operator to operations supervisor. He assisted in the pageantry for the 1960 Olympic Winter Games in Squaw Valley in California and the Disney attractions for the New York World's Fair in 1964. Sullivan relocated to Florida to help open Walt Disney World and remained there as an executive in operations until his retirement in 1993. He was named a Disney Legend in 2005.

WALKER, E. CARDON ("CARD") (1916–2005)
He served as president of Walt Disney Productions from 1971 to 1980 and chairman of the board from 1980 to 1983. He originally began with the company in 1938 delivering the mail, and worked his way up in the company in the camera and story departments, finally moving into advertising. In 1956 he was named vice president of advertising and sales, and he joined the board of directors in 1960. In 1965 he was appointed vice president of marketing. He became executive vice president and chief operating officer in 1968. It was Walker who, with Donn Tatum, ably led the company after Roy O. Disney's death, and who, in 1975, announced plans to commence with Walt's plans for EPCOT. He was elected president in 1971 and became chief executive officer in 1976. In this capacity, he oversaw its design and construction of EPCOT. In 1980 he was named chairman of the board. He retired in 1983 after supervising the opening of EPCOT Center, Tokyo Disneyland, and the launch of The Disney Channel. He remained on the company's board of directors until 1999, qualifying for his 50-year service award in 1988. He received the Disney Legend award in 1993.

Compiled by Graciela Loza, MLIS

DISNEYLANDMARKS

IMPORTANT DATES IN DISNEYLAND HISTORY

DECEMBER 5, 1901—Walt's birthday

NOVEMBER 18, 1928—Mickey and Minnie's debut in *Steamboat Willie*

JULY 13, 1955—Walt and Lilly's thirtieth wedding anniversary, held in Frontierland

JULY 17, 1955—Disneyland's Opening Day (Invitational Press Preview)

JULY 18, 1955—Disneyland opened to the public

JUNE 14, 1959—Disneyland's first major expansion: Matterhorn Bobsleds, Submarine Voyage, and Disneyland-Alweg Monorail debut debut.

OCTOBER 14, 1966—Walt's last day at Disneyland

JULY 2, 1967—New Tomorrowland celebrates its grand opening

DECEMBER—Candlelight Processional and Ceremony—The holiday tradition started by Walt in 1958 is generally held the first weekend in December.

Newspaper boy in front of Disneyland ticket booths and main entrance, 1955. The headline reads "Mickey Mouse Club Circus to Open Here." The short-lived attraction (November 1955–January 1956) under the world's largest striped circus tent featured Professor Keller and His Feline Fantastics, Serenado the Wonder Horse, Bob-O the Disneyland clown, and the Mouseketeers.

FROM MARCY

When I was a child, my grandparents took me one day each summer to Disneyland; it was always my favorite day of the year. Walt's sentiments in his 1955 Disneyland dedication speech ring truer than ever for me: Disneyland is my land. It's my source of joy and inspiration. And my purpose in writing this book.

There are many to thank, beginning with my mentor and my friend, Disney Legend Jim Cora. (AKA my "intern," a moniker Jim gave himself with his characteristic sense of humor.) We shared the same passion and commitment to preserving Walt's legacy in Disneyland. Jim was my trusted advisor; he opened the doors and made the introductions that were integral to my Disney career.

It was Jim, while we were having lunch at our favorite spot (Byblos Cafe in Orange, California, just a few miles from Disneyland), who insisted I write this book and to make it a priority over other projects. After Jim passed in March 2021, I knew the highest honor I could bestow was dedicating *Walt's Disneyland* to him. I do it with love, gratitude, and tremendous respect.

Working with Disney Editions is a dream come true. For my editor and friend, Wendy Lefkon, we've flown a few more kites since *Eat Like Walt*. Thank you for your steadfast support, collaboration, and brilliance, not to mention accommodating my perfectionism. Monica Vasquez, the managing editor with the *mostest*, I'm in awe of your quiet and fierce efficiency. Thank you for keeping this all on track. And Lindsay Broderick for always having her eyes on the design. Plus, copy editors Jennifer Black, Warren Meislin, and Rachel Rivera, who took my words (and gaffes) and made them perfect on the page.

Suzi Hutsell (of Cameron + Company)— brava!!! Your design is magical and magnificent! Thank you for your talent, grace and can-do attitude. Additionally at Cameron + Company, Iain Morris and Chris Gruener.

Everyone at Walt Disney Archives was challenged during the pandemic without direct access to the physical assets. Yet somehow, they pulled it off: Mike Buckhoff, thank you for your diligence sourcing and scanning images. You went above and beyond! Kevin M. Kern, you are a joy to work with; I appreciate your sage and gentle guidance. Ed Ovalle, your quiet and thoughtful wisdom is priceless. And Becky Cline, gratitude always for the behind-the-scenes support.

I'm also indebted to several others:

Graciela Loza, MLIS, for meticulously creating and compiling the endnotes and Dream Doer biographies. Paula Sigman Lowery for her professional counsel to us both.

Bri Bertolaccini and Caitlin Moneypenny-Johnston at The Walt Disney Family Museum for digging into their collection and helping me better tell Walt's Disneyland story.

Also invaluable for their contributions: Kaye Malins and the Walt Disney Hometown Museum in Marceline, Missouri.

For taking great care of me while I was working away from home: Jorge, Mike, and Leo at the Anaheim Marriott. Elmer at the GCH Craftsman Grill; Joe and the gang at Napa Rose.

My trusted early readers, Imagineers Kathy Mangum and Tom Fitzgerald.

Janet Ridgway for gifting me part of her father's collection. Cynthia Jones— a stranger— who generously gave me her copy of *World of Flowers* when she learned I was researching this book.

At Stonestreet Farm, my writing sanctuary in 2020: Barbara Banke, Lesley Howard, Ashley Sebastian, Doug Reynolds, Reid Becker, Kristin Miller, Sheri and Louie Logan, chef Amber Hruska, Daniel Cox, and the security staff.

Laura Jowdy, Sharon Edgington, and the Congressional Medal of Honor Society. Cris Piquinela at Curtis Publishing. Ashley Thomas and Rebecca Dupont at National Geographic. Paula Potter and Estella Moreno for the screen capture of Walt in the orange groves. Dana Morgan for the Arrow Development photos.

A heartfelt thank you to others who lent a helping hand: Aileen Kutaka in the IRC. Didier Ghez, editor of *Walt's People*. David Stern at WDI. Stephen Hall at the University of Arizona College of Pharmacy. Christopher Merritt. Rolly and Marie Crump. Kim Irvine. Tom K. Morris. Tony Baxter. Tania McKnight Norris. Peggie Fariss. Sandi Baldwin. Jonny Quest. Sean Bautista. Joseph Titizian. Denise Preskitt. At Disneyland's Flag Retreat, Susan Manskar Emslie and Marine Corps Sgt. Ernie "Gunny" Napper. My soul sibling Andrew Koenigsberg.

And for Walt: that feeling I have each and every time I'm in Disneyland . . . that feeling I share with millions and millions of people— thank you!!!

Walt captured during a rare moment of repose in Tomorrowland. Marty Sklar remarked, "You never saw Walt like this," 1956.

Walt, his characters, and children in front of Sleeping Beauty Castle, 1964.

ENDNOTES

INTRODUCTION

Walt used to say that . . . Roy Disney, "Unforgettable Walt Disney," *Reader's Digest*, February 1969, 218.

And I kept insisting I . . ." Walt Disney, "Speech at Tencennial Dinner at Disneyland Hotel" (Anaheim, CA, July 17, 1965), (WDA).

Operations supervisors' radios were instantly . . . Jim Cora, interview with author, February 26, 2019. See also, William "Sully" Sullivan, "Sully Remembers Walt Disney," in *From Jungle Cruise Skipper to Disney Legend: 40 Years of Magical Memories at Disney* (United States: Theme Park Press, 2015), 113.

I've always said there will . . ." Dave Smith, "On the Parks," in *The Quotable Walt Disney* (Los Angeles: Disney Editions, 2001), 74.

CHAPTER ONE: BEFORE DISNEYLAND

By the time Walt gets . . ." "How to Make a Buck," *Time*, July 1957.

He called the artist on . . . The Imagineers, "Chapter 1: The Spark," in *Imagineering: A Behind the Dreams Look at Making the Magic Real* (New York: Hyperion, 1996), 15.

Walt paced around the room . . ." "Three: Fantasy Lands & Disney Worlds," *A Brush with Disney: An Artist's Journey Told Through the Words and Works of Herbert Dickens Ryman*, ed. Bruce Gordon and David Mumford, research by Irene Naoum (Santa Clarita, CA: Camphor Tree Publishers, 2000), 143–147.

This whole area was just . . ." *Walt Disney's Wonderful World of Color*, "The Disneyland Tenth Anniversary Show," directed by Hamilton S. Luske, special material by Bill Berg, aired January 3, 1965, Walt Disney Productions.

I'm most proud that I . . ." "Three: Fantasy Lands & Disney Worlds," in *A Brush with Disney: An Artist's Journey Told Through the Words and Works of Herbert Dickens Ryman*, ed. Bruce Gordon and David Mumford, research by Irene Naoum (Santa Clarita, CA: Camphor Tree Publishers, 2000), 149.

Walt restlessly prowls the earth . . ." Bill Davidson, "The Fantastic Disney," *The Saturday Evening Post*, November 1964, 71.

In his first meeting with . . . Harrison "Buzz" Price, "Working with Walt and Roy," in *Walt's Revolution!: By the Numbers*, (Orlando: Ripley Entertainment, 2004), 27.

And with those marching orders . . . Harrison "Buzz" Price, "Working with Walt and Roy," 28.

Walt and Roy agreed with . . . See previous note.

I first saw the site . . ." Walt Disney, "Today and Tomorrow," *The Los Angeles Times* (Los Angeles, CA), June 14, 1965.

When he started Disneyland, I . . ." Lillian Disney, EPCOT Center interview by Bob Allen Jr., 1982 (WDA).

Walt's daughter Diane Disney Miller . . . Diane Disney Miller, as told to Pete Martin, "My Dad, Walt Disney: Conclusion," *The Saturday Evening Post*, January 1957, 81.

Walt sums it up: . . . "Disneyland U.S.A. at Radio City Music Hall," *Walt Disney Treasures: Your Host Walt Disney – TV Memories 1956–1965* (1962; Burbank, CA): Buena Vista Home Entertainment (2006), DVD.

The name Imagineering was suggested . . ." Marty Sklar, "Chapter 6: Just Do Something People Like—Walt Disney," in *Dream It! Do it!: My Half Century Creating Disney's Magic Kingdoms* (New York: Disney Editions, 2013), 50.

The key to Walt's approach . . ." Amy Boothe Green and Howard E. Green, "A King in His Magic Kingdom," in *Remembering Walt: Favorite Memories of Walt Disney* (New York: Hyperion, 1999), 156.

CHAPTER TWO: OUTSIDE DISNEYLAND

For all the people that . . ." Wally Boag and Gene Sand, "Disneyland," in *Wally Boag: Crown Prince of Disneyland* (New York: Disney Editions, 2009), 104.

Disneyland was closed on various . . . Dave Smith, "Disneyland," in *Disney Facts Revealed: Answers to Fans' Curious Questions* (Los Angeles: Disney Editions, 2016), 78.

A lover of all animals . . . Cecil Smith, "Walt Rides Magic Carpet Toward Greater, Never-Finished Disneyland," *The Los Angeles Times* (Los Angeles, CA), April 28, 1957.

Disneyland itself is the one . . ." Don Peri, "Van France," in *Working with Walt: Interviews with Disney Animators, Producers, and Artist* (Jackson, MS: The University Press of Mississippi, 2011), 143.

Disneyland is a state of . . ." Jim Bennett, "30 Million People Later," *The Los Angeles Herald Examiner* (Los Angeles, CA), June 17, 1962.

He told his operations team . . . Dick Nunis, *The Disneyland Philosophy*, 1983 (WDA).

The overall shape of the . . ." "Planning the First Disney Park: A Talk with Marvin Davis," *The "E" Ticket*, no. 28 (1997): 12.

One time he came over . . ." David Lesjak, "William Rast," in *Walt's People: Talking Disney with the Artists Who Knew Him*, ed. Didier Ghez, (United States: Xlibris, 2008), Volume 7: 18.

Ken-L Land (for the . . . Dave Smith, *Disney A to Z: The Official Encyclopedia*, 5th ed. (Los Angeles: Disney Editions, 2016), 417.

CHAPTER THREE: THE GRAND ENTRANCE

One thing that surprises me . . ." Cecil Smith, "Walt Rides Magic Carpet Toward Greater, Never-Finished Disneyland," *The Los Angeles Times* (Los Angeles, CA), April 28, 1957.

The story of Mickey is . . ." *Walt Disney's Disneyland*, season 1, episode 1, "The Disneyland Story," directed by Robert Florey and Wilfred Jackson, written by Bill Walsh, aired October 27, 1954, Walt Disney Productions.

It was also Walt's intention . . . Dick Irvine, interview with Richard Hubler, May 14, 1968 (WDA).

Walt peeks into the cockpit of his Disneyland-Alweg Monorail, 1959. Since it's a Highway in the Sky, "pilots" operate the vehicles.

While his film audiences traditionally . . . Bill Evans, "Introduction," in *Walt Disney Disneyland World of Flowers* (Burbank: Walt Disney Productions, 1965), 3.

Disneyland is the star: everything . . ." Dave Smith, "On the Parks," 57.

Here you leave today and . . ." *Disneyland Dictionary*, 1959 (WDA).

Fill this place with people . . ." Bob Thomas, "Foreground," in *Walt Disney: An American Original*, (New York: Disney Editions, 1976, 1994), 14.

CHAPTER FOUR: TOWN SQUARE
To all who come to . . ." Walt Disney, as quoted in *Dateline Disneyland*, American Broadcasting Company, Airdate: July 17, 1955 (WDA).

Walt welcomed his guests with . . . Walt Disney Productions, *Walt Disney's Guide to Disneyland* (New York: Disney Productions, 1964), 2.

SANTA FE AND DISNEYLAND RAILROAD AND MAIN STREET STATION (1955)
Los Angeles Times columnist Hedda . . . Hedda Hopper, "Disneyland Preview Reveals Wonderland," *The Los Angeles Times* (Los Angeles, CA), July 16, 1955.

In the earliest discussions for . . . Van Romans, interview with Les Perkins and Peggie Farris, 1987 (WDA).

Walt, you see, he had . . ." Herb Ryman, interview, July 22, 1987 (WDA).

Bill, people aren't soldiers!" Walt . . . Jeff Kurtti, "Chapter 3: The Place Makers," in *Walt Disney's Imagineering Legends and the* Genesis *of the Disney Theme Park* (New York: Disney Editions, 2008), 40.

Marvin Davis adds, "It was . . ." Van Romans, interview with Les Perkins and Peggie Farris, 1987 (WDA).

Or, as Walt said, "to . . ." Van Romans, interview with Les Perkins and Peggie Farris, 1987 (WDA).

Walt recounted, One day in . . ." Walt Disney, "I Have Always Loved Trains," *Railroad Magazine*, October 1965, 13.

So did his brother Roy: . . . Roy Disney, "Unforgettable Walt Disney," *Reader's Digest*, February 1969, 214.

Walt said proudly, "If you . . ." Walt Disney, "The Marceline I Knew," *The Marceline News* (Marceline, MO), September 2, 1938.

As an adult, he commuted . . . "About Marceline," *Walt Disney Hometown Museum*, accessed February 9, 2021, https://waltdisneymuseum.org/marceline/.

After he had achieved success . . . Roy Disney, "Unforgettable Walt Disney," 217.

Walt retired his home railroad . . . Bill Davidson, "The Fantastic Disney," 74.

Walt continued, "I'm going to . . ." Walt Disney, "I Have Always Loved Trains," 16.

TOUR GARDENS
She shares, "Walt really liked . . ." "Disney Legends: Cicely Rigdon." *D23: The Official Disney Fan Club*. Disney, accessed February 9, 2021. https://d23.com/walt-disney-legend/cicely-rigdon/.

He quipped, "This is a . . ." *Walt Disney's Wonderful World of Color*, "The Disneyland Tenth Anniversary Show," directed by Hamilton S. Luske, special material by Bill Berg, aired January 3, 1965, Walt Disney Productions.

DISNEYLAND CITY HALL (1955)
Imagineer Harper Goff explains that . . . "An Interview with Harper Goff," *The "E" Ticket*, no.14 (1992–93): 7.

City Hall also provided the . . . Rolly Crump, interview with author, January 18, 2019.

WALT'S APARTMENT (1955)
Disneyland was being built while . . ." "Diane Disney Miller: Remembering Dad," *Lady and the Tramp*, directed by Clyde Geronimi, Wilfred Jackson, Hamilton Luske, Jack Cutting (1955; Burbank, CA): Buena Vista Home Entertainment, (2012), Blu-Ray.

He said, "My wife and . . . Hedda Hopper, "Dream of Disneyland Still Being Realized," *The Los Angeles Times* (Los Angeles, CA), July 9, 1957.

Diane elaborates: "Mother and Dad . . ." "Diane Disney Miller: Remembering Dad," *Lady and the Tramp*, directed by Clyde Geronimi, Wilfred Jackson, Hamilton Luske, Jack Cutting (1955; Burbank, CA): Buena Vista Home Entertainment, (2012), Blu-Ray.

When dad would travel, they'd . . ." See previous note.

Diane describes the Disneyland residence . . . "Diane Disney Miller: Remembering Dad," *Lady and the Tramp*, directed by Clyde Geronimi, Wilfred Jackson, Hamilton Luske, Jack Cutting (1955; Burbank, CA): Buena Vista Home Entertainment, (2012), Blu-Ray.

It was their refuge; it . . ." Jordan Zakarin, "Diane Disney Remembers Her Dad: Walt's Secret Disneyland Apartment, His Passions & More," *HuffPost* (blog), February 7, 2012, https://www.huffpost.com/entry/walt-disneys-secret-disneyland-apartment-diane-disney-miller_n_1259421?-guccounter=1&guce_referrer=aHR0cHM6Ly93d3cuZ-29vZ2xlLmNvbS8&guce_referrer_sig=AQAAAB7EGluT-wv8f55vgFDg_sU6UI-IQW02JyFFBbX102qqq_YBSTKy-kijdoVei87H1rofAMurkeYM8ZCzkP05b5E55m5YTdm8B-fqDip8IDF1tufSBdg7dYnwkJGez1jKEh1wTc24Xc44k-R1BdmaCRJ3hBi4SN3O3JefEFu_m1bSyQUb.

Very private. It was for . . ." See previous note.

He told them how to . . ." Jordan Zakarin, "Diane Disney Remembers Her Dad: Walt's Secret Disneyland Apartment, His Passions & More," *HuffPost* (blog), February 7, 2012.

She remembers: "On the opening . . ." Amy Boothe Green and Howard E. Green, "Origins of Disneyland," in *Remembering Walt: Favorite Memories of Walt Disney* (New York: Hyperion, 1999), 153.

Walt cared about everyone. He . . ." Doug Lipp, "Lesson 4: Gather Facts and Feelings," in *Disney U: How Disney University Develops the World's Most Engaged, Loyal, and Customer-Centric Employees* (New York: McGraw-Hill, 2013), 57.

Herb Ryman talks about a . . . Herb Ryman, interview with Tony Baxter and Peggie Farris, 1987 (WDA).

Diane recalls, "He could watch . . ." "Diane Disney Miller: Remembering Dad," *Lady and the Tramp*, directed by Clyde Geronimi, Wilfred Jackson, Hamilton Luske, Jack Cutting (1955; Burbank, CA): Buena Vista Home Entertainment, (2012), Blu-Ray.

William "Sully" Sullivan, who started . . . William "Sully" Sullivan, "Sully Remembers Walt Disney," in *From Jungle Cruise Skipper to Disney Legend: 40 Years of Magical Memories at Disney* (United States: Theme Park Press, 2015), 112.

FLAG RETREAT CELEBRATION (1955)
He'd watch the flag lowering . . ." Diane Disney, EPCOT Center interview by Bob Allen Jr., 1982 (WDA).

He was a fierce patriot . . . Hedda Hopper Papers, Margaret Herrick Library, Academy of Motion Picture Arts and Sciences, Beverly Hills, CA.

To all of you that . . ." Recorded narration, Flag retreat ceremony, Disneyland Park, November 19, 2019.

BANK OF AMERICA (1955)/DISNEY GALLERY (2009)
The first bank on Town . . ." *Spirit of Disneyland*, Folder Walt Disney Production Through 1989, Clipping Files Collection, IRC, Walt Disney Imagineering, Glendale, California.

While they had helped to . . . *Spirit of Disneyland*, Folder Walt Disney Production Through 1989, Clipping Files Collection, IRC, Walt Disney Imagineering, Glendale, California.

OPERA HOUSE (1955)
The first building finished at. . . Courtesy of the Walt Disney Hometown Museum.

His daughter Diane says, "I . . ." Diane Disney Miller, interview with Richard Hubler, June 11, 1968 (WDA).

As you enter the lobby . . . Dave Smith, "On the Parks," 51.

GREAT MOMENTS WITH MR. LINCOLN (1966)
It was like working on . . ." "Designing Disneyland with Marc Davis," *The "E" Ticket*, no. 7 (1989): 10.

In the fifth grade, he . . . Jeffrey Moffit, "Look Closer: Great Moments with Mr. Lincoln," *The Walt Disney Family Museum* (blog), March 1, 2013, https://www.waltdisney.org/blog/look-closer-great-moments-mr-lincoln.

Walt continued to portray the . . . "Man of the Week - - - Walt Disney," *The Akron Beacon Journal* (Akron, Ohio), November 17, 1940.

Walt had been mulling the idea . . . Bill Davidson, "The Fantastic Disney," 71.

Harriet Burns recollected, "In the . . . "Flair and Versatility: A Visit to Walt's Original W.E.D. Model Shop with Harriet Burns," *The "E" Ticket*, no. 44, (2006): 39.

Everything that Walt Disney believed . . . Dick Nunis, *The Disneyland Philosophy*,1983 (WDA).

Walt was very involved with . . . *Walt Disney's Wonderful World of Color*, "Disneyland Goes to the World's Fair," directed by Hamilton S. Luske, narration written by Charles Shows, aired May 17, 1964, Walt Disney Productions.

Imagineer Roger Broggie adds that . . . Roger Broggie, attraction documentation (WDA).

Walt further challenged his Imagineers . . . Gereon Zimmermann, "World's Fair: Showcase of Our Times Opens April 22," *Look*, February 1964, 31.

We didn't present the Gettysburg . . ." Walt Disney, *Great Moments with Mr. Lincoln Attraction Training Guide*, 1964.

He's going to be very . . ." Walt Disney, interview by Fletcher Markle, Canadian Broadcasting Corporation, September 25, 1963 (WDA).

Walt felt that Great Moments . . . "Great Moments with Mr. Lincoln," Disneyland University (WDA).

So that young people may . . ." See previous note.

It has taken me three . . ." Attraction documentation (WDA).

Herb Ryman recalls, "It was . . ." Don Peri, "Herb Ryman," in *Working with Walt: Interviews with Disney Artists* (Jackson, MS: The University Press of Mississippi, 2008), 172.

Lloyd might have been unaware . . . See previous note.

DISNEYLAND'S VEHICLES
OMNIBUS (1956)
Imagineer Bob Gurr, who says . . . "Disneyland's Main Street Omnibus," *The "E" Ticket*, no. 40 (2003): 14.

The park means a lot . . ." Bob Thomas, "Chapter 20," in *Walt Disney: An American Original* (New York: Disney Editions, 1976, 1994), 244.

Sometimes he'd just come down . . ." Amy Boothe Green and Howard E. Green, "A King in His Magic Kingdom," 166.

One time I spotted that . . . "Disneyland's Main Street Omnibus," *The "E" Ticket*, no. 40 (2003): 14.

When he came back, he . . . See previous note.

HORSELESS CARRIAGES (1956)
When it was decided that . . . "Main Street Horseless Carriage Debuts at Disneyland." *D23: The Official Disney Fan Club*. Disney. Accessed February 9, 2021, https://d23.com/this-day/main-street-horseless-carriage-debuts-at-disneyland/.

HORSE-DRAWN STREETCARS (1955)
Regarding the short walking distance . . . Ira Wolfert, "Walt Disney's Magic Kingdom," *Reader's Digest*, April 1960, 145.

FIRE ENGINE (1958)
Walt's response was "You're right . . ." "Main Street Fire Engine Celebrates 55 Years at Disneyland Park," *Disney Parks Blog* (blog) August 16, 2013, https://disneyparks.disney.go.com/blog/2013/08/main-street-fire-engine-celebrates-55-years-at-disneyland-park/.

CANDLELIGHT CEREMONY AND PROCESSIONAL
This beloved Christmastime tradition began . . . Joseph Titizian, "The Season of Giving: Walt and the Candlelight Processional," *The Walt Disney Family Museum* (blog), December 12, 2011, https://www.waltdisney.org/blog/season-giving-walt-and-candlelight-processional.

WALT AND TRASH
When I started on Disneyland . . ." Dave Smith, "On the Parks," 47.

Yep. That was him . . ." Orlando Ferrante, interview with author, May 10, 2018.

Always setting an example for . . ." Ron Miller, interview with author, April 24, 2016.

CHAPTER FIVE: MAIN STREET, U.S.A.
Many of us fondly remember . . ." Walt Disney Productions, *Walt Disney's Pictorial Souvenir Book of Disneyland* (New York: Disney Productions, 1958), n.p.

He oft repeated, "More things . . ." "About Marceline," *Walt Disney Hometown Museum*, accessed February 9, 2021, https://waltdisneymuseum.org/marceline/.

Walt added his whimsy to . . . Ira Wolfert, "Walt Disney's Magic Kingdom," 145–146.

Walt spent weeks and weeks . . ." Herb Ryman, interview with Tony Baxter and Peggie Farris, 1987 (WDA).

I said, 'What are you . . ." See previous note.

WEST SIDE
EMPORIUM (1955)
This is another building based . . . Courtesy of The Walt Disney Hometown Museum.

At the time Walt's U.S. postage stamp was approved, the United States Postal Service required that a person be deceased ten years before they could be eligible. Walt, however, was an exception. His stamp was issued in his hometown of Marceline less than two years after he passed away.

Walt and his authentic Ice . . . Bob Gurr, interview with author, March 4, 2016.

And I know more adults . . ." Dave Smith, "On Children, Young and Old," in *The Quotable Walt Disney*, (Los Angeles; New York: Disney Editions, 2001), 129.

The Emporium along with the . . . The Imagineers, "Main Street U.S.A.: Start Your Day with a Visit to Yesteryear," in *The Imagineering Field Guide to Disneyland: An Imagineer's-Eye Tour* (New York: Disney Editions, 2008), 24.

Often he squatted down and . . ." Bob Thomas, "Chapter 22," in *Walt Disney: An American Original* (New York: Disney Editions, 1976, 1994), 266.

In Walt's day, the Emporium . . . Ira Wolfert, "Walt Disney's Magic Kingdom," 152.

A family caught my attention . . . Jack Lindquist with Melinda J. Combs, "Chapter 7: Winter Wonderland" in *In Service to the Mouse: My Unexpected Journey to Becoming Disneyland's First President* (Orange: Chapman University Press, 2010), 24–25.

ELIAS DISNEY WINDOW (1955)
The 1895 date on the . . . "Windows on Main Street, U.S.A., at Disneyland Park: Elias Disney," *Disney Parks Blog* (blog), June 13, 2013, https://disneyparks.disney.go.com/blog/2013/06/windows-on-main-street-u-s-a-at-disneyland-park-elias-disney/.

It's often repeated that he . . . Walt Disney, interview by Pete Martin for *The Saturday Evening Post*, c. 1956/1957. Courtesy of The Walt Disney Family Museum.

MAIN STREET U.S.A. TRIBUTE WINDOWS
Imagineer Harper Goff explains further . . . "Main Street: Walt's Perfect Introduction to Disneyland," *The "E" Ticket*, no. 14 (1992–93): 33.

THE FORUOUSITY SHOP—FORMERLY UPJOHN PHARMACY (1955–1970)
Upjohn's director of advertising Jack . . . *Disneyland's Upjohn Pharmacy*, History of Pharmacy Museum, The University of Arizona, Tucson, AZ.

Main Street in Disneyland reminds . . ." Diane Disney Miller, as told to Pete Martin, "My Dad, Walt Disney: Hard Times in Kansas City," *The Saturday Evening Post*, November 1956, 70.

CARNATION CAFÉ (1955)
Sometimes he'd sip a milkshake . . . Oscar Martinez, interview with author, February 25, 2016.

Like most people, I have . . ." Walt Disney Productions, *Walt Disney's Pictorial Souvenir Book of Disneyland* (New York: Disney Productions, 1968), n.p.

He liked them runny. A . . ." Oscar Martinez, interview with author, February 25, 2016.

One of Disneyland's first hires . . . Amy Boothe Green and Howard E. Green, "A King in His Magic Kingdom," 158.

The tribute window above the . . . Kevin Kern, "What's in a Name?—Renie Conley, Costumer to the Stars—Part One," *D23: The Official Disney Fan Club*, March 16, 2020, https://d23.com/whats-in-a-name-renie-conley-costumer-to-the-stars-part-one/.

Dear Mr. Disney: May I . . ." Renie Conley to Walt Disney, August 01, 1955, Walt Disney Correspondence collection (WDA).

GIBSON GIRL ICE CREAM PARLOR—FORMERLY SUNKIST CITRUS HOUSE (1960–1989)
In the wee hours of . . . Marcy Carriker Smothers, "Chapter 3: Walt's Disneyland: Main Street, U.S.A.," *Eat Like Walt: The Wonderful World of Disney Food* (Los Angeles: Disney Editions, 2017), 64.

Pretty soon it occurred to . . . See previous note.

While that was considerate, Walt . . ." Amy Boothe Green and Howard E. Green, "A King in His Magic Kingdom," 160.

Those oranges had more than . . . Rolly Crump, interview with author, March 9, 2019.

I love to visit there . . ." Vernon Scott, "Disneyland Plans to Add Many Animals," *The New Castle News* (New Castle, PA), April 29, 1960.

COCA-COLA REFRESHMENT CENTER (1955)
Or as former attraction host . . . Jim Cora, interview with author, January 17, 2019.

THE PAVILION (1955–1963)
JOLLY HOLIDAY (2015)
It was here that John . . . John Hench with Peggy Van Pelt, "The Art of the Show," in *Designing Disney: Imagineering and the Art of the Show* (New York: Disney Editions, 2003), 30.

Walt tells us, "Other people . . ." Amy Boothe Green and Howard E. Green, "A King in His Magic Kingdom," 158.

This location was briefly Stouffer's . . . Marcy Carriker Smothers, "Chapter 3: Walt's Disneyland: Main Street, U.S.A.," 74–75.

Disneyland is often called a . . ." Dave Smith, "On the Parks," 62.

In Hall's book *When You* **. . .** Joyce C. Hall with Curtiss Anderson, "More Than a Sunday Painter," *When You Care Enough: The Story of Hallmark Cards and Its Founder* (Kansas City, MO: Hallmark Cards, 1979), 131.

EAST SIDE
MAIN STREET CINEMA (1955)
Inside the box office the . . . Kaye Malins, interview with author, February 27, 2019.

Walt wore his heart on . . . Gereon Zimmermann, "World's Fair: Showcase of Our Times Opens April 22," 32.

Walt explains, "Our first sound . . ." *Disneyland*, "The Story of the Animated Drawing," directed by Wilfred Jackson and William Beaudine, written by Dick Huemer and McLaren Stewart, aired November 30, 1955, Walt Disney Productions.

MARKET HOUSE (1955)
Evoking the feel of yesteryear . . . Bob Thomas, "Chapter 21," in *Walt Disney: An American Original* (New York: Disney Editions, 1976, 1994), 258.

CENTER STREET (1955)
WATER FOUNTAIN
This is not just another . . . Center Wall on Main Street Photo (1955). Courtesy of Joseph Titizian.

HOTEL MARCELINE
Although Walt wasn't likely to . . . Joe Fowler, interview with Bob Thomas, 1973 (WDA).

SWIFT'S RED WAGON INN (1955–1965)
PLAZA INN (1965)
Walt insisted on fine furnishing . . . Elaine Woo, "Emile Kuri; Oscar-Winning Designer Worked on Disneyland," *The Los Angeles Times* (Los Angeles, CA), October 13, 2000.

Walt had intended to have . . . *Walt Disney's Wonderful World of Color*, "The Disneyland Tenth Anniversary Show," directed by Hamilton S. Luske, special material by Bill Berg, aired January 3, 1965, Walt Disney Productions.

HIDEOUT (1955 AND 1965)
From the earliest planning document . . . Marcy Carriker Smothers, "Chapter 3: Walt's Disneyland: Main Street, U.S.A.," 68.

However, with the Plaza Inn's . . . Tom K. Morris, email message to author, August 1, 2019.

POPCORN PEOPLE
I caught sight of a . . ." Jack Jungmeyer, "Under the Gaslights," *The Disneyland News* 1, no.1 (1985): 3.

WALT AND WALKING
Like a kid with a new . . ." Roy Disney, "Unforgettable Walt Disney," *Reader's Digest*, February 1969, 217.

Father does more walking than . . ." Diane Disney Miller, "Chapter 14," *The Story of Walt Disney* (New York: Disney Editions, 1957), 22.

I think that's probably the . . ." Courtesy of The Walt Disney Family Museum.

Walt would regularly walk through. . ." Van Arsdale France, "Deadline Days," in *Window on Main Street: 35 Years of Creating Happiness at Disneyland Park* (United States: Theme Park Press, 2015), 39.

I was so astonished by the . . ." Amy Boothe Green and Howard E. Green, "A King in His Magic Kingdom," 156.

He walked fast and expected . . ." Charles Ridgway, "Chapter 2," in *Spinning Disney's World: Memories of a Magic Kingdom Press Agent* (Branford, CT: Intrepid Traveler, 2007), 15.

That was the only park . . ." Marty Sklar, *Orange County Register*, 1991.

CHAPTER SIX: THE HUB
To walk from Town Square . . ." Martin Sklar, *Walt Disney's Disneyland*, (Anaheim, CA: Walt Disney Productions, 1969), 3.

He explained to Herb Ryman. . . *Disney Family Album*, "Disneyland Designers," directed by Michael Bonifer, written by Jim Fanning, aired December 7, 1984.

I planned it so each . . ." Bob Thomas, "Foreground," in *Walt Disney: An American Original* (New York: Disney Editions, 1976, 1994), 13.

The more I go to . . ." Bob Thomas, "Disney Keeps on Building His Fantasyland," *The Kansas City Times* (Kansas City, MO), November 2, 1964.

SLEEPING BEAUTY CASTLE
In a meeting with fellow . . . Todd James Pierce, "And Still Nothing Is Built," in *Three Years in Wonderland: The Disney Brothers, C. V. Wood, and the Making of the Great American Theme Park* (Jackson, MS: The University Press of Mississippi, 2016), 125.

At that moment Walt Disney . . ." Herb Ryman, interview with Tony Baxter and Peggie Farris, 1987 (WDA).

On this occasion, he looked . . . Ray Bradbury, "Why Disney Will Live Forever," in *Mickey Is Sixty!* (New York: Time Inc., 1988), 48.

He called John Hench at . . . See previous note.

Walt is Mickey. If Mickey . . ." Walt Disney, "The Cartoon's Contribution to Children," *Overland Monthly*, October 1933, 138.

PARTNERS **STATUE**
The *Partners* **statues in the . . .** William "Sully" Sullivan, "Sully Remembers Walt Disney," 112.

His interpretation of Walt on . . ." See previous note.

Blaine remarked of his masterpiece . . . Michael Broggie and Gary Oakland, "Marvin Davis and Marjorie Davis," in *Walt's People: Talking Disney with the Artists Who Knew Him*, ed. Didier Ghez, (United States: Theme Park Press, 2020), Volume 24: 197.

I think what I want . . ." Dave Smith, "On Children Young and Old," 138.

A KISS GOODNIGHT
Enthusiasm and optimism together. He . . ." Lillian Disney, interview by Richard Hubler, April 16, 1968.

He called the tradition "a . . ." Richard M. Sherman and Brittany Rubiano, "The Birth of a Song," in *A Kiss Goodnight* (Los Angeles: Disney Editions, 2017), n.p.

Songwriter Richard Sherman ran into . . . See previous note.

DISNEYLANDSCAPES
Walt said, 'I went in . . ." "An Interview with Harper Goff," *The "E" Ticket*, no.14 (1992–93): 10–11.

Yesterday it was a peaceful . . . Hedda Hopper, "Disneyland Shrubs, Trees Cost $400,000," *The Los Angeles Times* (Los Angeles, CA), May 23, 1955.

Walt wanted each tree to . . ." Bob Thomas, "Chapter 22," in *Walt Disney: An American Original* (New York: Disney Editions, 1976, 1994), 264.

Walt Disney wanted a 'green' . . ." Ruth Patricia Shellhorn, "Disneyland-Dream Built in One Year Through Team Work of Many Artist," *Landscape Architecture*, April 1956, 134.

Chlorophyll Characters. Walt saw topiary . . ." *Vacationland,* Fall/Winter 1982–83.

Remember when we opened, if . . ." Walt Disney, "Speech at Tencennial Dinner at Disneyland Hotel" (Anaheim, CA, July 17, 1965), (WDA).

Disneyland was a huge success . . ." Ward Kimball, interview with Rick Shale, January 29, 1976 (WDA).

At Disneyland a jungle must . . ." Bill Evans, *Walt Disney Disneyland World of Flowers* (Burbank: Walt Disney Productions, 1965), 3.

It was a miracle Disneyland . . . "Art Linkletter and Dateline Disneyland," *The "E" Ticket*, no. 40 (2003): 10.

Not only can I add things . . ." Dave Smith, "On the Parks," 57.

In the year before Disneyland . . . The Imagineers, "Chapter 4: Making It Real," in *Imagineering: A Behind the Dreams Look at Making the Magic Real* (New York: Hyperion, 1996), 156.

Below the station, on the . . . Ruth Patricia Shellhorn, "Disneyland-Dream Built in One Year Through Team Work of Many Artist," 134.

CHAPTER SEVEN: ADVENTURELAND
Everyone has a dream of . . ." Walt Disney Productions, *Walt Disney's Guide to Disneyland* (New York: Disney Productions, 1964), 22.

WALT DISNEY'S ENCHANTED TIKI ROOM (1963)
Harriet Burns recalled Walt's vision . . . Harriet Burns, interview with Scott Wolf, Mouse Clubhouse, January 17, 2008 (WDA).

She observed, "So Walt had . . ." Pete Docter and Christopher Merritt, "Chapter 5: Walt Disney's Enchanted Tiki Room," in *Marc Davis in His Own Words: Imagineering the Disney Theme Parks* (Glendale, CA: Disney Editions, 2019), Volume 1: 116.

After it was over, we . . ." *The Imagineering Story*, "The Happiest Place on Earth," directed by Leslie Iwerks, written by Mark A. Catalena, narrated by Angela Bassett, aired November 12, 2019, Iwerks & Co. Production.

Well, our reaction was absolute . . ." See previous note.

Luckily we remembered that about . . ." Robert B. Sherman and Richard M. Sherman, "Walt's Time," in *Walt's Time: From Before to Beyond* (Santa Clarita, CA: Camphor Tree, 1998), 32.

I want the skippers to . . ." Doug Lipp, "Lesson 3: It Takes Art and Science," in *Disney U: How Disney University Develops the World's Most Engaged, Loyal, and Customer-Centric Employees* (New York: McGraw-Hill, 2013), 44.

This is the latest thing . . ." Robert de Roos, "The Magic Worlds of Walt Disney," *National Geographic* 124, no. 2 (1963): 202.

It's just animation with sound . . ." See previous note.

Walt explained in detail: "It's . . ." Robert de Roos, "The Magic Worlds of Walt Disney," 202.

You know, the same scientific . . ." Pete Docter and Christopher Merritt, in "Chapter 5: Walt Disney's Enchanted Tiki Room," in *Marc Davis in His Own Words: Imagineering the Disney Theme Parks*, Volume 1: 118.

Walt with guests on the Skyway, 1956.

We operate fifteen hours a . . ." Walt Disney, interview by Fletcher Markle, Canadian Broadcasting Corporation, September 25, 1963 (WDA).

When Walt was asked if . . . Robert de Roos, "The Magic Worlds of Walt Disney," 202.

JUNGLE CRUISE (1955)
Walt's brother-in-law and . . . Bill Cottrell, interview with Richard Hubler, March 12, 1968 (WDA).

Blaine Gibson explains what happened . . . "Walt Disney's Sculptor Blaine Gibson," *The "E" Ticket*, no. 21 (1995): 19.

Imagineer Sam McKim adds more . . . *Walt: The Man Behind the Myth*, directed by Jean-Pierre Isbouts (2001; Burbank, CA): Walt Disney Home Video, (2001), DVD.

Bob Thomas recalls the early . . . Amy Boothe Green and Howard E. Green, "Origins of Disneyland," 151.

We're going to have an . . ." Charles Witbeck, "Walt Disney Plans TV Shows a Year Ahead," *The Asbury Park Press* (Monmouth County and Ocean County, NJ), February 9, 1963.

Just listening to him talk . . ." Charles Ridgway, "Chapter 4," in *Spinning Disney's World: Memories of a Magic Kingdom Press Agent* (Branford, CT: Intrepid Traveler, 2007), 121.

Giraffes, you can see them . . ." Amy Boothe Green and Howard E. Green, "Origins of Disneyland," 151.

In Walt's mind, the whole . . ." Amy Boothe Green and Howard E. Green, "Origins of Disneyland," 151.

Dick Nunis, who held many . . . Creating Happiness for Walt, Clipping Files Collection, IRC, Walt Disney Imagineering, Glendale, California.

Walt was the first to . . ." Amy Boothe Green and Howard E. Green, "A King in His Magic Kingdom," 155.

After he left, I got . . ." Creating Happiness for Walt, Clipping Files Collection, IRC, Walt Disney Imagineering, Glendale, California.

DOMINGUEZ FAMILY TREE (1895)
Landscape designer Bill Evans shares . . . Bill Evans, "Adventureland," in *Walt Disney Disneyland World of Flowers* (Burbank: Walt Disney Productions, 1965), 56.

When the owner of the . . . See previous note.

SWISS FAMILY TREEHOUSE (1962)
RE-THEMED AS TARZAN'S TREEHOUSE (1999)
Every kid has had dreams . . ." *Walt Disney's Wonderful World of Color*, "The Disneyland Tenth Anniversary Show," directed by Hamilton S. Luske, special material by Bill Berg, aired January 3, 1965, Walt Disney Productions.

Betty Taylor, one of the stars . . . Amy Boothe Green and Howard E. Green, "A King in His Magic Kingdom," 160.

Shortly thereafter a reporter from . . . "The Wide World of Walt Disney," *Newsweek*, December 1962, 51.

When I was a youngster . . ." Jim Bennett, "30 Million People Later," *The Los Angeles Herald Examiner* (Los Angeles, CA), June 17, 1962.

I built things in the . . ." Edith Efron, "Still Attacking His Ancient Enemies—Conformity," *TV Guide*, July 1965, 11.

WALT'S DISGUISES AND BEING RECOGNIZED IN DISNEYLAND
You know . . . I know people . . ." Jim Bennett, "30 Million People Later," *The Los Angeles Herald Examiner* (Los Angeles, CA), June 17, 1962.

When Walt toured around Disneyland . . ." Ken Anderson, interview with Richard Hubler, "Audio-Animatronics and Disneyland," March 26, 1968, 5 (WDA).

When Mother and Father visit . . ." Diane Disney Miller, "Chapter 14," in *The Story of Walt Disney* (New York: Disney Editions, 1957), 224–225.

Someone told me a great . . ." Wally Boag and Gene Sand, "Disneyland," 79.

He spent his time going . . ." Jim Korkis, "Ken Anderson," in *Walt's People: Talking Disney with the Artists Who Knew Him*, ed. Didier Ghez, (United States: Xlibris, 2008), Volume 6: 245.

When we first arrived in . . ." Amy Boothe Green and Howard E. Green, "A King in His Magic Kingdom," 156.

CHAPTER EIGHT: FRONTIERLAND
Here you can return to . . . *Walt Disney's Guide to Disneyland* (New York: Walt Disney Productions, 1964), 14.

FRONTIERLAND PLAQUE AND FLAGPOLE (1955)
Walt's care and concern for . . . Edith Efron, "Still Attacking His Ancient Enemies—Conformity," *TV Guide*, July 1965, 12.

He loved the little animals . . ." Don Peri, "Herb Ryman," in *Working with Walt: Interviews with Disney Artists* (Jackson, MS: The University Press of Mississippi, 2008), 159.

One morning before the park . . ." Jim Cora, interview with author, January 17, 2019.

THE GOLDEN HORSESHOE (1955)
Prior to the attraction's debut . . . Don Peri, "Herb Ryman," in *Working with Walt: Interviews with Disney Artists* (Jackson, MS: The University Press of Mississippi, 2008), 159.

I can't remember how many . . ." Wally Boag and Gene Sand, "Disneyland," 118.

As the festivities kept going . . . Wally Boag and Gene Sand, "Introduction," in *Wally Boag: Crown Prince of Disneyland* (New York: Disney Editions, 2009), viiii.

People below started to notice him . . . Bob Thomas, "Chapter 22," in *Walt Disney: An American Original* (New York: Disney Editions, 1976, 1994), 271.

THE OTHER OCCUPIED APARTMENT AT DISNEYLAND
He explains, "Walt was so . . ." Wally Boag and Gene Sand, "Disneyland," 120.

THE RIVERS OF AMERICA (1955)
I think he took more . . ." Marvin Davis, interview with Richard Hubler, May 28, 1968 (WDA).

When the time came to . . ." Wilfred Jackson, interview with Richard Hubler, March 26, 1968 (WDA).

Walt said, 'No, just cut . . .' See previous note.

Disney Parks Publicist Charles Ridgeway . . . Charles Ridgway, "Chapter 4," in *Spinning Disney's World: Memories of a Magic Kingdom Press Agent* (Branford, CT: Intrepid Traveler, 2007), 38.

Sometimes he'd sit with his . . ." Marty Sklar, interview with author, February 25, 2016.

Renie Bardeau, the photographer famous . . . Renie Bardeau, interview with Scott Wolf, *Mouse Clubhouse Conversation*, November 20, 2019.

MARK TWAIN RIVERBOAT (1955)
Come on, Roland. Let's go . . ." Rolly Crump, interview with author, January 18, 2019.

Rolly remembers vividly, "We boarded . . . See previous note.

Everyone in the park knew . . ." *Disney Family Album*, "WED Imagineers," directed by Larry Smoot, aired June 13, 1985.

If he was working, he'd . . ." William "Sully" Sullivan, "Sully Remembers Walt Disney," in *From Jungle Cruise Skipper to Disney Legend: 40 Years of Magical Memories at Disney* (United States: Theme Park Press, 2015), 110.

FOWLER'S HARBOR (1955)
By the time Joe gets . . ." Joe Fowler, interview with Jay Horan, March 12, 1984 (WDA).

Joe Fowler, who retired from the . . . See previous note.

Yes, he loved it. There . . ." Joe Fowler, interview with Richard Hubler, July 23, 1968 (WDA).

No steamship that ever plied . . ." Don Peri, "Herb Ryman," in *Working with Walt: Interviews with Disney Artists* (Jackson, MS: The University Press of Mississippi, 2008), 159.

TOM SAWYER ISLAND (1956)
Imagineer Marvin Davis recalls the . . . Marvin Davis, interview with Richard Hubler, May 28, 1968 (WDA).

Walt said gleefully, "I put . . ." Ira Wolfert, "Walt Disney's Magic Kingdom," 147.

I was originally called upon . . ." *The Imagineering Story*, "The Happiest Place on Earth", directed by Leslie Iwerks, written by Mark A. Catalena, narrated by Angela Bassett, aired November 12, 2019, Iwerks & Co. Production, Disney+.

Years after Walt passed away . . . Jack Lindquist with Melinda J. Combs, "Chapter 30: Recreating Walt's Childhood," in *In Service to the Mouse: My Unexpected Journey to Becoming Disneyland's First President* (Orange: Chapman University Press, 2010), 103.

FISHING PIER (1956–CIRCA MID-1960S)
Joe Fowler explains that the . . . Joe Fowler, interview with Richard Hubler, July 23, 1968 (WDA).

The river was stocked with . . . Ron Dominguez, interview with author, January 14, 2016.

its demise in part the . . . See previous note.

Walt's sailing ship was accomplished . . . The Imagineers, "Frontierland," in *The Imagineering Field Guide to Disneyland: An Imagineer's-Eye Tour* (New York: Disney Editions, 2008), 51.

WALT'S DREAMING TREE IN THE LOKOTA VILLAGE
Nestled behind the large tepee . . . Kim Irvine, interview with author, July 14, 2019.

One was replanted near the . . . Kaye Malins, interview with author, August 20, 2020.

The third was gifted to . . . See previous note.

SAILING SHIP *COLUMBIA* (1958)
Typical is what happened one . . ." Roy Disney, "Unforgettable Walt Disney," 218.

Walt chose the *Columbia* for . . . "Disneyland Launches Replica of *Columbia*: Full-Scale Model of First American Ship to Circle Globe Makes Maiden Voyage," *The Los Angeles Times* (Los Angeles, CA), June 15, 1958.

During construction Walt was fascinated . . ." Joe Fowler, interview with Jay Horan, March 12, 1984 (WDA).

Upon its debut, Walt proudly . . . *Walt Disney's Wonderful World of Color*, "The Disneyland Tenth Anniversary Show," directed by Hamilton S. Luske, special material by Bill Berg, aired January 3, 1965, Walt Disney Productions.

CASA DE FRITOS (1957–1982)
RANCHO DEL ZOCALO (2001)
This building was erected for . . . Marcy Carriker Smothers, "Chapter 5: Walt's Disneyland: Frontierland," in *Eat Like Walt: The Wonderful World of Disney Food* (Los Angeles: Disney Editions, 2017), 107.

The miniature buildings were . . . Jeff Kurtti, "Chapter 3: The Place Makers," in *Walt Disney's Imagineering Legends and the Genius of the Disney Theme Park* (New York: Disney Editions, 2008), 42.

PIONEER MERCANTILE (1955)
Walt purchased several coin-operated . . . Kevin Quon, "A Historic Musical Gem," *Parker & Goff Weekly* 16, no. 4 (2016): n.p.

Mrs. Raney was quite particular . . . See previous note.

PETRIFIED TREE (1957)
Charlie Ridgway recalls the day . . . Charles Ridgway, "Chapter 7," in *Spinning Disney's World: Memories of a Magic Kingdom Press Agent* (Branford, CT: Intrepid Traveler, 2007), 58.

PANCAKE HOUSE (1955–1970)
RIVER BELLE TERRACE (1971)
According to Walt's daughter Diane . . . "Diane Disney Miller: Remembering Dad," *Lady and the Tramp*, directed by Clyde Geronimi, Wilfred Jackson, Hamilton Luske, Jack Cutting (1955; Burbank, CA): Buena Vista Home Entertainment, (2012), Blu-Ray.

FRONTIERLAND TRAIN STATION (1955–1966)
Jim Cora shares a fun . . . Jim Cora, interview with author, January 17, 2019.

Disneyland's original Tom Sawyer, Tom . . . Amy Boothe Green and Howard E. Green, "A King in His Magic Kingdom," 160.

WALT'S SKETCHING AND DOODLING
As usual, he was sketching . . ." The Autopia: Disneyland's "Expressway of the Future"," *The "E" Ticket*, no. 27 (1997): 31.

When we would go out . . ." Lillian Disney, EPCOT Center interview by Bob Allen Jr., 1982 (WDA).

Walt would often draw on . . ." Ron Miller, interview by author, September 1, 2016.

Walt was very interested in . . ." "Planning the First Disney Park: A Talk with Marvin Davis," *The "E" Ticket*, no. 28 (1997): 11.

Disney Legend and Walt Disney . . . Dave Smith, *Disney A to Z: The Official Encyclopedia*, 5th ed. (Los Angeles: Disney Editions, 2016), 507.

CHAPTER NINE: NEW ORLEANS SQUARE
Disneyland has always had a . . . *Walt Disney's Wonderful World of Color*, "Disneyland Around the Seasons," directed by Hamilton S. Luske, narration written by Larry Clemmons, aired December 18, 1966, Walt Disney Productions.

Herb Ryman recalls Walt's impatience . . . "Three: Fantasy Lands & Disney Worlds," in *A Brush with Disney: An Artist's Journey Told Through the Words and Works of Herbert Dickens Ryman*, ed. Bruce Gordon and David Mumford, research by Irene Naoum (Santa Clarita, CA: Camphor Tree Publishers, 2000), 180.

Thanks to Herb, Bill Martin . . . *Walt Disney's Wonderful World of Color*, "Disneyland Around the Seasons," directed by Hamilton S. Luske, narration written by Larry Clemmons, aired December 18, 1966, Walt Disney Productions.

Walt continued, "And all these . . ." *Walt Disney's Wonderful World of Color*, "The Disneyland Tenth Anniversary Show," directed by Hamilton S. Luske, special material by Bill Berg, aired January 3, 1965, Walt Disney Productions.

It kind of started with . . ." Pete Docter and Christopher Merritt, in "Chapter 5: Walt Disney's Enchanted Tiki Room," in *Marc Davis in His Own Words: Imagineering the Disney Theme Parks* (Glendale, CA: Disney Editions, 2019), Volume 1: 97.

Walt knew every nail in . . . Courtesy of The Walt Disney Family Museum.

PIRATES OF THE CARIBBEAN (1967)
This is a Caribbean town . . ." *Walt Disney's Wonderful World of Color*, "The Disneyland Tenth Anniversary Show," directed by Hamilton S. Luske, special material by Bill Berg, aired January 3, 1965, Walt Disney Productions.

Buoyed by the success at . . . Becky Cline and Rob Klein. "A Toast to New Orleans," *Disney twenty-three*, Fall 2009, 36–38.

Walt was very clear to . . . The Imagineers, "Chapter 3: Blood, Sweat, and Tears," in *Imagineering: A Behind the Dreams Look at Making the Magic Real* (New York: Hyperion, 1996), 118.

Imagineer X Atencio remembers, "We . . ." Amy Boothe Green and Howard E. Green, "A King in His Magic Kingdom," 165.

Marc Davis adds, "Walt was . . ." "A Marc Davis Pirates Sketchbook," *The "E" Ticket*, no. 32 (1999): 14.

Walt made the final decision . . . "Pirates of the Caribbean: More Gems From This Disney Treasure," *The "E" Ticket*, no. 32 (1999): 27.

Walt tasked Herb Ryman: "Now . . ." Herb Ryman, interview with Tony Baxter and Peggie Farris, 1987 (WDA).

WALT AND ROY'S APARTMENT
He explained to his pal . . . Wally Boag and Gene Sand, "Disneyland," 143.

BLUE BAYOU RESTAURANT (1967)
Shortly thereafter Walt abandoned the . . . Becky Cline and Rob Klein. "A Toast to New Orleans," *Disney twenty-three*, Fall 2009, 36–38.

All of us who worked . . ." Steven Langlois and Epcot Discovery Center, "Partners:' A Lasting Legacy for the Magic Kingdom and Imagineer Blaine Gibson," *Walt Disney World Eyes & Ears* 25, no. 38 (1995):1 & 4.

CLUB 33 (1967)
Walt Disney's concept—an . . . Club 33 Membership Sales Brochure, Walt Disney Productions, 1967.

Tania recalls, "My days were . . ." Tania McKnight Norris, interview by author, January 31, 2021.

Walt had a personal space . . . Marcy Carriker Smothers, "Chapter 8: Walt's Last Land: New Orleans Square," 137.

The idea was basic magic . . . See previous note.

Jim Cora, then a supervisor . . . Jim Cora, interview with author, January 17, 2019.

Walt's grandson and namesake, Walter . . . Jenny Goff, interview with author, September 1, 2016.

CREOLE CAFÉ (1966)
RENAMED CAFÉ ORLEANS (1972)
Cast members Sally Hames and . . . Sally Hames and

Jo Anne Wheeler, "Candid Corner," *Backstage Disneyland*, Spring 1967, 18 (WDA).

HAUNTED MANSION (1969)
I'm told I'm not supposed . . . Bob Thomas, "Hollywood," *Santa Cruz Sentinel* (Santa Cruz, CA), March 22, 1957.

While he didn't live to . . . Ed Squair, interview by Kurtti-Pellerin, "Haunted Mansion/Pirates of the Caribbean," March 2003 (WDA).

Walt's playful way with the macabre . . . Walt Disney, "Speech at Welcome Home Reception" (Marceline, MO, July 1956), Walt Disney Hometown Museum, https://fb.watch/4oJ5kjYNNC/.

Harriet Burns adds, "They just . . ." Harriet Burns, interview by Kurtti-Pellerin, "Haunted Mansion/Pirates of the Caribbean," March 15, 2003, 17 (WDA).

I don't want anything ghostly . . ." Harriet Burns, interview by Kurtti-Pellerin, "Haunted Mansion/Pirates of the Caribbean," March 15, 2003, 20–21 (WDA).

Walt's directive to Marc Davis . . . "Designing Disneyland with Marc Davis," *The "E" Ticket*, no. 7 (1989): 14.

Harriet burns recalls, "We built . . ." Amy Boothe Green and Howard E. Green, "A King in His Magic Kingdom," 166.

If you asked six different . . ." Jim Korkis, "Ken Anderson," in *Walt's People: Talking Disney with the Artists Who Knew Him*, ed. Didier Ghez, (United States: Xlibris, 2008), Volume 6: 256.

Walt wanted it to be . . ." Pete Docter and Christopher Merritt, in "The Haunted Mansion: Part 1," in *Marc Davis in His Own Words: Imagineering the Disney Theme Parks* (Glendale, CA: Disney Editions, 2019), Volume 1: 340.

Later, on his television show . . . *The Imagineering Story*, "What Would Walt Do?," directed by Leslie Iwerks, written by Mark A. Catalena, narrated by Angela Bassett, aired November 15, 2019, Iwerks & Co. Production.

Although Walt had passed away . . . Frees, Paul. "The Genius of Paul Frees," *Haunted Mansion 30th Anniversary* (Red Dot Net, 1999), compact disc (WDA).

CHAPTER TEN: FANTASYLAND
What youngster hasn't dreamed of . . ." Randy Bright, "Heigh-Ho, Heigh-Ho, It's Off to Work We Go," in *Disneyland: Inside Story* (New York: Harry N. Abrams, Inc. Publishers, 1987), 81.

This may be because it . . . "Fantasyland," in *Walt Disney's Guide to Disneyland* (New York: Walt Disney Productions, 1964), 8.

KING ARTHUR CARROUSEL (1955)
A merry-go-round was . . ." "King Arthurs Carrousel," *The "E" Ticket*, no. 35 (2001): 7.

SNOW WHITE'S ADVENTURES (1955)
SNOW WHITE'S SCARY ADVENTURES (1983)
We received water from every . . . Jack Lindquist with Melinda J. Combs, "Chapter 23: It is a Small World After All," in *In Service to the Mouse: My Unexpected Journey to Becoming Disneyland's First President* (Orange: Chapman University Press, 2010), 75.

Walt personally named each of . . . Diane Disney Miller, as told to Pete Martin, "My Dad, Walt Disney: Disney's Folly," *The Saturday Evening Post*, December 1956, 81.

Art Director Ken Anderson, whom . . . Walt Disney Archives/Ken Anderson Files.

Walt once put it simply: . . ." Dave Smith, "On Children, Young and Old," 131.

PINOCCHIO'S DARING JOURNEY (1983)
Whenever I go on a . . ." Dave Smith, "On the Parks," 53.

CASEY JR. CIRCUS TRAIN (1955)
This was initially conceived as . . . The Imagineers, "Fantasyland: Storybooks Come to Life in the Most Magical Land of All," in *The Imagineering Field Guide to Disneyland: An Imagineer's-Eye Tour* (New York: Disney Editions, 2008), 88.

That was one of the . . ." Joe Fowler, interview with Jay Horan, March 12, 1984 (WDA).

Joe delivered the disappointing news . . . See previous note.

DUMBO THE FLYING ELEPHANT (1955)
Dumbo the Flying Elephant was . . . The Imagineers, "Fantasyland: Storybooks Come to Life in the Most Magical Land of All," in *The Imagineering Field Guide to Disneyland: An Imagineer's-Eye Tour* (New York: Disney Editions, 2008), 83.

MR. TOAD'S WILD RIDE (1955)
Inspired by *The Adventures of* . . . Randy Bright, "Heigh-Ho, Heigh-Ho, It's Off to Work We Go," in Disneyland: Inside Story (New York: Harry N. Abrams, Inc. Publishers, 1987), 81.

Mr. Toad has an interesting . . . Amy Boothe Green and Howard E. Green, "A King in His Magic Kingdom," 163.

PETER PAN'S FLIGHT (1955)
Bob Thomas observed about this . . . Bob Thomas, "Chapter 22," in *Walt Disney: An American Original* (New York: Disney Editions, 1976, 1994), 265.

If Walt said, 'WOW!' it . . ." Van Arsdale France, "The Walt Disney School of Trial-and-Error Management," in *Window on Main Street: 35 Years of Creating Happiness at Disneyland Park* (United States: Theme Park Press, 2015), 76.

MAD TEA PARTY (1955)
NEW LOCATION (1983)
The Mad Tea Party is a gaily colored . . ." Walt Disney Productions, *Walt Disney's Pictorial Souvenir Book of Disneyland* (New York: Disney Productions, 1965), n.p.

ALICE IN WONDERLAND (1958)
Walt never lost his enthusiasm . . . Walt Disney, "My Newest Dream," *The American Weekly*, March 1958, 8.

CANAL BOATS OF THE WORLD (1955)
STORYBOOK LAND CANAL BOATS (1956)
When time permitted, Walt assisted . . . Marcel Bonner and Stephen Daly, "Remembering Fred Joerger: Master of Miniatures and Mountain," *The "E" Ticket*, no. 44 (2006): 9.

When I was doing those . . ." "Flair and Versatility: A Visit to Walt's Original W.E.D. Model Shop with Harriet Burns," *The "E" Ticket*, no.44, (2006): 33.

Dick Nunis commented on Walt's . . . Amy Boothe Green and Howard E. Green, "A King in His Magic Kingdom," 163.

"it's a small world" (1966)
NEW YORK WORLD'S FAIR (1964–1965)
Walt had a clear vision . . . Pete Docter and Christopher Merritt, in "Chapter 7: The 1964–65 New York World's Fair Part 2: General Electric Carousel of Progress and "it's a small world"," in *Marc Davis in His Own Words: Imagineering the Disney Theme Parks* (Glendale, CA: Disney Editions, 2019), Volume 1: 195.

Walt's original idea was to . . . Tom Fitzgerald, email message to author, November 5, 2020.

Walt was quick and to . . . Robert B. Sherman and Richard M. Sherman, "Walt's Time," in *Walt's Time: From Before to Beyond* (Santa Clarita, CA: Camphor Tree, 1998), 36.

Richard Sherman adds, "We wrote . . . See previous note.

Walt said that I knew . . ." John Canemaker, *The Art and Flair of Mary Blair* (New York: Disney Editions, 2003, rev. 2014), 19.

Rolly Crump ensured Mary's significant . . . Rolly Crump, interview with author, March 9, 2019.

When she queried Walt as . . . Pete Docter and Christopher Merritt, in "Chapter 7: The 1964–65 New York World's Fair Part 2: General Electric Carousel of Progress and "it's a small world"," Volume 1: 222.

Rolly suggested bands could play . . . Rolly Crump, interview with author, January 18, 2019.

Later, when Walt looked at . . . See previous note.

When the facade and clock . . . *Walt Disney's Wonderful World of Color*, "Disneyland Around the Seasons," directed by Hamilton S. Luske, narration written by Larry Clemmons, aired December 18, 1966, Walt Disney Productions.

MATTERHORN BOBSLEDS (1959)
Walt returned from visiting the . . . The Imagineers, "Fantasyland: Storybooks Come to Life in the Most Magical Land of All," in *The Imagineering Field Guide to Disneyland: An Imagineer's-Eye Tour* (New York: Disney Editions, 2008), 92.

Bob Gurr was given the . . . *The Imagineering Story*, "The Happiest Place on Earth," directed by Leslie Iwerks, written by Mark A. Catalena, narrated by Angela Bassett, aired November 12, 2019, Iwerks & Co. Production.

Joe Fowler supervised the construction . . . Joe Fowler, interview with Jay Horan, March 12, 1984 (WDA).

The track itself was not . . ." See previous note.

As soon as I had . . ." Joe Fowler, interview with Jay Horan, March 12, 1984 (WDA).

You might see that down . . ." Becky Cline, "Walt's Great Adventures with Becky Cline" (Zoom presentation, Bowers Museum, Santa Ana, CA, March 6, 2021).

ARROW AND WALT
Bob Gurr, who worked closely . . . Bob Gurr, "Walt's Team—WED and the Imagineers," in *Bob Gurr: Legendary Imagineer: Life and Times—Disney and Beyond* (Middletown: Independently Published, 2019), 72.

SNOW WHITE'S GROTTO (1961)
When the Carrara marble sculpts . . . The Imagineers, "Fantasyland: Storybooks Come to Life in the Most Magical Land of All," in *The Imagineering Field Guide to Disneyland: An Imagineer's-Eye Tour* (New York: Disney Editions, 2008), 90.

The ideas of Walt Disney . . . Ruth Patricia Shellhorn, "Disneyland: Dream Built in One Year Through Teamwork of Many Artist, *Landscape Architecture*, April 1956, 134.

SNOW WHITE'S WISHING WELL (1961)
When John Hench showed him . . . John Hench with Peggy Van Pelt, "The Art of Visual Storytelling," in *Designing Disney: Imagineering and the Art of the Show* (New York: Disney Editions, 2003), 77.

SKYWAY TO TOMORROWLAND (1956–1994)
Prompted by a report from . . . Emile Kuri to Walt Disney, Walt Disney Productions Inter-Office Communication, July 29, 1958 (WDA).

Walt sent a memo to . . . Walt Disney to Park Operations Committee, Walt Disney Productions Inter-Office Communication, July 31, 1958 (WDA).

Walt rides the Mine Train Through Nature's Wonderland (among his favorite attractions) with his grandchildren, 1960.

WALT, WAITING, AND CROWD CONTROL
I've always been conscious of . . ." Don Alpert, "The Man of the Land Disney," *The Los Angeles Times* (Los Angeles, CA), April 30, 1961.

At 'small world' [at the . . ." William "Sully" Sullivan, "The 1964 New York World's Fair Story," in *From Jungle Cruise Skipper to Disney Legend: 40 Years of Magical Memories at Disney* (United States: Theme Park Press, 2015), 49.

So we stood in the . . . See previous note.

To control crowds at the . . . Charles Ridgway, "Chapter 2," in *Spinning Disney's World: Memories of a Magic Kingdom Press Agent* (Branford, CT: Intrepid Traveler, 2007), 11.

In the early days of . . ." Jim Cora, interview with author, January 17, 2019.

He usually stands in line . . . *The Saturday Evening Post.*

And people control is one . . ." Jay Rogers, "The Park That Imagination Built. Fantastic Disneyland Gets Better Every Year," *The San Antonio Express* (San Antonio, TX), May 16, 1965.

CHAPTER ELEVEN: TOMORROWLAND
Tomorrow can be a wonderful . . ." Walt Disney Productions, *Walt Disney's Pictorial Souvenir Book of Disneyland* (New York: Disney Productions, 1965), n.p.

Walt famously quipped, "Tomorrow is . . ." Walt Disney, "Welcome remarks at Congressional Medal of Honor Reception" (Anaheim, CA, October 14, 1966), The Walt Disney Archives.

ROCKET TO THE MOON (1955–1966)
Astronaut was hardly a household . . . *Walt Disney's Disneyland*, "Man in Space," directed by Ward Kimball, written by Ward Kimball and William Bosche, aired March 9, 1955, Walt Disney Productions.

The round trip of about . . . Walt Disney, "Land of Tomorrow: You can Take a Trip to the Moon," *The American Weekly*, July 1955, 17.

FLIGHT TO THE MOON (1967–1975)
Ten years later, Walt was . . . Louis Berg, "Walt Disney's New Ten Million Dollar Toy," *This Week*, September 1954, 8.

PEOPLEMOVER (1967–1995)
I'm not against the automobile . . ." Walt Disney, Florida Press Conference, November 15, 1965 (WDA).

Bob Gurr recalls, "We were . . ." "The Autopia: Disneyland's "Expressway of the Future"," *The "E" Ticket*, no. 27 (1997): 31.

MARY BLAIR MURALS
On the way over we . . ." Dick Irvine, interview with Richard Hubler, May 14, 1968 (WDA).

Those tiles were covered . . . Dave Smith, "Disneyland" in *Disney Facts Revealed: Answers to Fans' Curious Questions* (Los Angeles: Disney Editions, 2016), 69.

MONSANTO HOUSE OF THE FUTURE (1957–1967)
Lilly's story about an encounter . . . Lilian Disney, interview with Bob Thomas, 1973 (WDA).

When we were designing the . . ." Pete Docter and Christopher Merritt, in "Cousin Orville," in *Marc Davis in His Own Words: Imagineering the Disney Theme Parks* (Glendale, CA: Disney Editions, 2019), Volume 1: 184.

WALT DISNEY'S CAROUSEL OF PROGRESS (1967–1973)
NEW YORK WORLD'S FAIR 1964–1965
Walt loved that Carousel of . . ." Marty Sklar, "Chapter 3, The New York World's Fair: From 'Menopause to Manor' to Flushing Meadows" in *Travels with Figment: On the Road in Search of Disney Dreams* (Glendale, CA: Disney Editions, 2019), 51.

He explained his latest innovation . . . "WED Enterprises, Inc. "For G.E." [promotional film]," *Walt Disney Treasures - Tomorrow Land: Disney in Space and Beyond*, directed by Hamilton Luske, and Ward Kimball (1963; Burbank, CA): Walt Disney Studios Home Entertainment, (2004), DVD.

Walt continued, "In act one . . ." *Walt Disney's Wonderful World of Color*, "Disneyland Goes to the World's Fair," directed by Hamilton S. Luske, narration written by Charles Shows, aired May 17, 1964, Walt Disney Productions.

There's a Great Big Beautiful . . . Robert B. Sherman and Richard M. Sherman, "Walt's Time," in *Walt's Time: From Before to Beyond* (Santa Clarita, CA: Camphor Tree, 1998), 34.

AUTOPIA (1955)
however, it was Walt who . . . Bruce Gordon. David Mumford. Roger Le Roque, and Nick Farago, "Chapter 2: The Little Parkway," in *Disneyland the Nickel Tour: A Postcard Journey Through a Half Century of the Happiest Place on Earth* (Santa Clarita, CA: Camphor Tree Publishers, 2000), 73.

Walt took one look and . . . Van Arsdale France, "Off to Tomorrowland," in *Window on Main Street: 35 Years of Creating Happiness at Disneyland Park* (United States: Theme Park Press, 2015), 64.

Bob Gurr reports, "A week . . ." The Imagineers, "Chapter 3: Blood, Sweat, and Tears,"113.

As Bob explained to him . . . "The Autopia: Disneyland's "Expressway of the Future"," *The "E" Ticket*, no. 27 (1997): 31.

TOMORROWLAND TERRACE (1967)
Well, let's put in an . . . " Dick Irvine, interview with Richard Hubler, May 14, 1968 (WDA).

MONORAIL (1959)
Bob Gurr recalls the serendipitous . . . *Walt: The Man Behind the Myth*, directed by Jean-Pierre Isbouts (2001; Burbank, CA): Walt Disney Home Video (2001), DVD.

Whenever he came into the . . ." Charles Ridgway, "Chapter 4," in *Spinning Disney's World: Memories of a Magic Kingdom Press Agent* (Branford, CT: Intrepid Traveler, 2007), 36.

I remember the meeting when . . ." Bob Gurr, "Early Days of the Monorail," *The "E" Ticket*, no. 36 (2001): 16.

SUBMARINE VOYAGE (1959)
FINDING NEMO SUBMARINE VOYAGE (2007)
Walt always strived for realism . . . "The First Quarter Century," in *Disneyland: The First Quarter Century* (Hollywood: Walt Disney Productions, 1979) 57.

After the attraction was completed . . . Walt Disney, "My Newest Dream," *The American Weekly*, March 1958, 8.

Walt later laminated the joke . . . Walt Disney, interview by Fletcher Markle, Canadian Broadcasting Corporation, September 25, 1963 (WDA).

A through C tickets were . . . Jack Lindquist with Melinda J. Combs, "Chapter 54: When Money Talks, Everyone Listens," in *In Service to the Mouse: My Unexpected Journey to Becoming Disneyland's First President* (Orange: Chapman University Press, 2010), 201.

SPACE MOUNTAIN (1977)
John Hench recalls Walt suggesting . . . John Hench, Folder The Art of Disneyland 1953–1986, Clipping Files Collection, IRC, Walt Disney Imagineering, Glendale, California.

Walt didn't call it Space . . ." John Hench, Folder Disneyland Line Space Mountain Edition, Clipping Files Collection, IRC, Walt Disney Imagineering, Glendale, California.

Walt wanted to build a . . ." John Hench with Peggy Van Pelt, "The Art of the Show," in *Designing Disney: Imagineering and the Art of the Show* (New York: Disney Editions, 2003), 12.

The plan was done about . . ." "Imagineering and the Disney Image: An Interview with Marty Sklar," *The "E" Ticket*, no. 30 (1998): 10.

We didn't just build this . . ." John Hench, Folder Disneyland Line Space Mountain Edition, Clipping Files Collection, IRC, Walt Disney Imagineering, Glendale, California.

RECLINATA TREE (1967)
Rolly Crump recalls that Bill . . . Rolly Crump, interview with author, January 18, 2019.

NIXON AND THE MONORAIL
My circle was getting larger . . ." Tony Baxter, interview with author, July 12, 2016.

On the first visit to . . . See previous note.

CHAPTER TWELVE: THE GRAND CIRCLE TOUR
You want to run it . . ." Jim Korkis, "Ward Kimball," in *Walt's People: Talking Disney with the Artists Who Knew Him*, ed. Didier Ghez, (United States: Xlibris, 2005), Volume 2:100.

In 1958 and 1959, two . . . George Savvas, "A Look Back: 1958 Opening of the Grand Canyon Diorama at Disneyland Park," *Disney Parks Blog* (blog), March 29, 2013, https://disneyparks.disney.go.com/blog/2013/03/a-look-back-1958-opening-of-the-grand-canyon-diorama-at-disneyland-park/.

Finally, there is one very . . . "A Train for Lilly," *Disney Parks Blog* (blog), February 9, 2010, https://disneyparks.disney.go.com/blog/2010/02/a-train-for-lilly/.

GRAND CANYON (1958)
Walt described the newest addition . . . Walt Disney, "My Newest Dream," *The American Weekly*, March 1958, 7–8.

Engine number three was put . . . George Savvas, "A Look Back: 1958 Opening of the Grand Canyon Diorama at Disneyland Park," *Disney Parks Blog* (blog), March 29, 2013, https://disneyparks.disney.go.com/blog/2013/03/a-look-back-1958-opening-of-the-grand-canyon-diorama-at-disneyland-park/.

PRIMEVAL WORLD (1966)
Walt announced details about an . . . "All New for '66!," *Disney News: Official Magazine for Magic Kingdom Club Families* 1, no. 3 (1966): 2.

Walt detailed the creation of . . . *Walt Disney's Wonderful World of Color*, "Disneyland Around the Seasons," directed by Hamilton S. Luske, narration written by Larry Clemmons, aired December 18, 1966, Walt Disney Productions.